# vegan Mexican co

A vegan culinary exploration of Mexican cuisine, Flavors of Compassion

Alonzo B. Obrien

# Table of Content

**Guacamole with Plantain Chips:** .................................................................. 13

**Spicy Salsa Verde with Homemade Tortilla Chips:** ............................................ 14

**Vegan Queso Fundido:** ............................................................................... 15

**Stuffed Jalapeno Poppers:** .......................................................................... 16

**Black Bean Nachos:** ................................................................................... 17

**Corn and Avocado Salsa:** ............................................................................ 19

**Grilled Street Corn with Vegan Crema:** .......................................................... 20

**Tofu Taquitos with Chipotle Sauce:** ............................................................... 21

**Vegan Ceviche:** ......................................................................................... 22

**Roasted Red Pepper and Walnut Dip:** ........................................................... 24

**Vegan Tortilla Soup:** .................................................................................. 25

**Spicy Lentil Pozole:** ................................................................................... 27

**Chipotle Black Bean Soup:** .......................................................................... 28

**Creamy Pumpkin and Corn Chowder:** ........................................................... 30

**Mexican Quinoa Chili:** ................................................................................ 31

**Roasted Tomato and Red Pepper Gazpacho:** .................................................. 33

Sopa de Fideos (Vegan Mexican Noodle Soup): ................................................. 34

Three-Bean Vegan Chili: .................................................................................... 36

Calabacitas Soup: .............................................................................................. 37

Pozole Verde with Jackfruit: .............................................................................. 38

Vegan Tacos al Pastor: ...................................................................................... 40

Mushroom and Spinach Enchiladas: ................................................................. 41

Cauliflower Tinga Tostadas: .............................................................................. 43

Vegan Chiles Rellenos: ...................................................................................... 44

Jackfruit Carnitas Burritos: ................................................................................ 45

Vegan Mole Poblano: ........................................................................................ 47

Tofu and Vegetable Fajitas: ............................................................................... 48

Vegan Tamales with Salsa Roja: ........................................................................ 50

Potato and Poblano Flautas: ............................................................................. 51

Stuffed Bell Peppers with Mexican Rice and Black Beans: ................................ 52

Mexican Rice with Charred Corn: ..................................................................... 54

Spicy Black Beans with Cilantro Lime Rice: ....................................................... 55

Vegan Refried Beans: ........................................................................................ 57

Chipotle Lime Quinoa: ...................................................................................... 58

Cumin-Scented Brown Rice: ............................................................................. 59

Coconut Cilantro Lime Rice: ............................................................................. 60

Pinto Bean and Rice Burrito Bowl: .................................................................... 61

Red Rice with Roasted Peppers: ................................................................................. 62

Vegan Black Bean and Corn Salad: .............................................................................. 63

Three-Bean Quinoa Salad: ........................................................................................... 64

Grilled Cactus Salad: .................................................................................................... 65

Jicama and Mango Slaw: .............................................................................................. 66

Roasted Sweet Potato and Avocado Salad: ................................................................. 67

Mexican Street Corn Salad: ......................................................................................... 68

Vegan Caesar Salad with Pepitas: ................................................................................ 69

Tomato and Avocado Salad with Lime Dressing: ........................................................ 71

Charred Zucchini with Cilantro and Lime: ................................................................... 72

Roasted Beet and Orange Salad: ................................................................................. 72

Spicy Pickled Red Onions: ............................................................................................ 73

Quinoa and Black Bean Stuffed Bell Peppers: ............................................................. 75

Creamy Chipotle Sauce: ............................................................................................... 76

Roasted Tomato Salsa: ................................................................................................. 77

Mango and Habanero Salsa: ........................................................................................ 78

Vegan Sour Cream with Lime: ..................................................................................... 79

Salsa Negra (Black Garlic Salsa): .................................................................................. 80

Cilantro Lime Crema: ................................................................................................... 81

Vegan Ranchero Sauce: ............................................................................................... 82

Pomegranate and Jalapeno Salsa: ............................................................................... 83

Roasted Tomatillo Salsa: ...................................................................... 84

Ancho Chili Cashew Cream: ................................................................ 85

Vegan Flour Tortillas: .......................................................................... 86

Blue Corn Tortillas: ............................................................................. 87

Sopes with Refried Beans and Guacamole: ........................................ 88

Vegan Conchas (Sweet Bread): ........................................................... 90

Cornbread with Green Chilies: ........................................................... 91

Pumpkin Seed Tortillas: ...................................................................... 93

Vegan Bolillos (Crusty Rolls): .............................................................. 94

Chia and Flaxseed Tortillas: ................................................................ 95

Vegan Tres Leches Cake: ..................................................................... 96

Sweet Potato Empanadas: .................................................................. 98

Vegan Churros with Chocolate Sauce: .............................................. 100

Coconut Tres Leches Cake: ............................................................... 102

Cinnamon-Sugar Buñuelos: .............................................................. 104

Vegan Arroz con Leche: .................................................................... 105

Chocolate Avocado Mousse: ............................................................ 107

Mango Sorbet with Chili-Lime Salt: .................................................. 108

Agua Fresca Popsicles (Horchata, Jamaica, Tamarind): ................... 109

Vegan Flan with Caramel Sauce: ...................................................... 110

Mexican Hot Chocolate Brownies: ................................................... 111

Vegan Pineapple Empanadas: ................................................................. 113

Classic Horchata: ..................................................................................... 115

Vegan Mexican Coffee: ........................................................................... 116

Hibiscus Tea (Agua de Jamaica): ............................................................. 117

Spicy Mango Margarita: .......................................................................... 118

Cucumber Lime Agua Fresca: .................................................................. 118

Vegan Piña Colada: .................................................................................. 119

Minty Mojito Mocktail: ............................................................................ 120

Mexican Hot Chocolate: ........................................................................... 120

Prickly Pear Cactus Smoothie: ................................................................. 121

Vegan Chilaquiles: .................................................................................... 122

Tofu Scramble Breakfast Tacos: ............................................................... 123

Sweet Potato and Black Bean Breakfast Burritos: ................................... 124

Vegan Breakfast Enchiladas: .................................................................... 126

Mexican-Inspired Avocado Toast: ............................................................ 127

Vegan Breakfast Quesadillas: ................................................................... 128

Chorizo-Spiced Tofu Breakfast Bowl: ....................................................... 129

Vegan Huevos Rancheros: ....................................................................... 130

Cinnamon-Sugar Churro Pancakes: .......................................................... 131

Mexican-Inspired Tofu Benedict: ............................................................. 132

Vegan Elote (Grilled Corn): ...................................................................... 134

Tofu and Vegetable Tlayudas: .................................................................... 135

Vegan Sopes with Pico de Gallo: ................................................................ 136

Spicy Mango with Chili Powder: ................................................................. 137

Vegan Tacos de Canasta: .......................................................................... 138

Vegan Gorditas: ...................................................................................... 140

Street-Style Roasted Nuts with Spices: ...................................................... 140

Vegan Quesadilla with Salsa Roja: ............................................................. 141

Churro Bites with Caramel Dipping Sauce: .................................................. 142

Vegan Day of the Dead Sugar Skull Cookies: ............................................... 144

Vegan Posadas Fruit Punch: ...................................................................... 145

Noche Buena Tamales: ............................................................................. 146

Vegan Christmas Pomegranate Guacamole: ................................................ 147

Vegan Cinco de Mayo Piña Colada Cupcakes: .............................................. 148

Vegan Día de los Muertos Pan de Muerto: .................................................. 150

Vegan Thanksgiving Enchiladas: ................................................................ 152

Vegan Hanukkah Potato Tacos with Vegan Sour Cream: ............................... 153

Vegan Independence Day Salsa Fireworks: ................................................. 154

Vegan Valentine's Day Chocolate Chili Truffles: ........................................... 155

Vegan Yucatan Tofu Tacos: ....................................................................... 156

Oaxacan-Style Vegan Mole Enchiladas: ...................................................... 158

Vegan Tamales de Elote (Corn Tamales): ................................................... 159

Vegan Chiles en Nogada: .................................................................. 160

Vegan Cochinita Pibil Tacos: .............................................................. 161

Vegan Enfrijoladas (Black Bean Enchiladas): ..................................... 162

Vegan Sopes de Chorizo de Soya: ..................................................... 163

Vegan Chicharrón en Salsa Verde: .................................................... 164

Vegan Guisado de Nopales (Cactus Stew): ........................................ 165

Vegan Chamorro de Borrego Tacos (Lamb Shank Tacos): ................. 166

Vegan Mexican Sushi Rolls: ............................................................... 167

Vegan Mexican-Inspired Pizza: .......................................................... 169

Tofu and Vegetable Fajita Stir-Fry: ................................................... 170

Vegan Mexican-Inspired Buddha Bowl: ............................................ 171

Vegan Mexican-Inspired Spring Rolls: ............................................... 172

Vegan Mexican-Inspired Grain Bowl: ................................................ 174

Vegan Mexican-Inspired Tofu Lettuce Wraps: .................................. 175

Jackfruit Carnitas Tostada Salad: ...................................................... 176

Vegan Mexican-Inspired Avocado Sushi: .......................................... 177

Mexican-Inspired Vegan Ramen: ...................................................... 178

Vegan Mexican Mac and Cheese: ..................................................... 179

Vegan Mexican-Inspired Shepherd's Pie: .......................................... 180

Vegan Mexican Chili Cheese Fries: .................................................... 181

Vegan Mexican-Inspired Stuffed Peppers: ........................................ 182

Vegan Mexican-Inspired Lasagna: ...................................................................... 183

Vegan Mexican-Inspired Goulash: .................................................................... 184

Vegan Mexican-Inspired Biscuits and Gravy: .................................................... 185

Vegan Mexican-Inspired Meatloaf: ................................................................... 186

Vegan Mexican-Inspired Pot Pie: ...................................................................... 187

Vegan Mexican-Inspired Breakfast Casserole: ................................................. 188

Vegan Grilled Portobello Fajitas: ...................................................................... 189

Vegan Mexican-Inspired Grilled Veggie Platter: ............................................... 191

Vegan Mexican-Inspired BBQ Skewers: ............................................................ 192

Grilled Tofu Tacos with Pineapple Salsa: .......................................................... 193

Vegan Mexican-Inspired BBQ Jackfruit Sandwiches: ........................................ 194

Vegan Mexican-Inspired Peanut Butter and Jelly Tortillas: .............................. 195

Vegan Mexican-Inspired Ants on a Log: ........................................................... 196

Vegan Mexican-Inspired Grilled "Cheese" Quesadilla: ..................................... 196

Vegan Mexican-Inspired Cauliflower "Wings": ................................................. 197

Vegan Mexican-Inspired Tofu Dino Nuggets: ................................................... 199

Vegan Mexican-Inspired Macaroni Salad: ........................................................ 200

Vegan Mexican-Inspired Pizza Bagels: .............................................................. 201

Vegan Mexican-Inspired Fruit Roll-Ups: ............................................................ 202

Vegan Mexican-Inspired Potato Smileys: ......................................................... 203

Vegan Mexican-Inspired Zucchini Noodles with Pico de Gallo: ........................ 205

Vegan Mexican-Inspired Stuffed Bell Peppers with Quinoa: ..........................205

Vegan Mexican-Inspired Avocado and Black Bean Salad: ...............................206

Vegan Mexican-Inspired Cucumber and Watermelon Salad: .........................208

Vegan Mexican-Inspired Chia Seed Pudding with Mango: ..............................208

Vegan Mexican-Inspired Green Smoothie Bowl:................................................209

Vegan Mexican-Inspired Black Bean and Corn Quinoa Salad: ........................210

Vegan Mexican-Inspired Chickpea Salad with Cumin Dressing:......................211

Vegan Mexican-Inspired Cauliflower Rice Bowl:...............................................212

Vegan Mexican-Inspired Grilled Veggie Wrap:..................................................213

Vegan Mexican-Inspired One-Pot Rice and Beans:...........................................214

Vegan Mexican-Inspired Sheet Pan Fajitas: ......................................................215

Vegan Mexican-Inspired 15-Minute Salsa Pasta: .............................................216

Vegan Mexican-Inspired Tofu Tacos in a Hurry:...............................................217

Vegan Mexican-Inspired Quick Guacamole Toast: ..........................................218

Vegan Mexican-Inspired Instant Pot Chili: .......................................................219

Vegan Mexican-Inspired 10-Minute Taco Salad: .............................................220

Vegan Mexican-Inspired Speedy Tofu Scramble: ............................................222

Vegan Mexican-Inspired Express Quinoa Burrito Bowl: .................................223

Vegan Mexican-Inspired Spaghetti with Salsa Marinara: ...............................224

Vegan Mexican-Inspired Sweet Potato and Black Bean Quesadilla: ..............225

Vegan Mexican-Inspired Jackfruit Sloppy Joes:...............................................226

Vegan Mexican-Inspired BBQ Chickpea Tacos: ...................................................227

Vegan Mexican-Inspired Tofu Nuggets with Dip: .............................................228

Vegan Mexican-Inspired Cheesy Zucchini Casserole: ......................................229

Vegan Mexican-Inspired Stuffed Mushroom Caps: ........................................230

Vegan Mexican-Inspired Potato and Poblano Tacos: ....................................231

Vegan Mexican-Inspired Kid-Friendly Burrito Bowl: .......................................231

Vegan Mexican-Inspired Mini Taco Salad Cups: .............................................232

Vegan Mexican-Inspired Portobello Tacos with Cilantro Pesto: ......................234

Vegan Mexican-Inspired Eggplant Mole Tower: ..............................................235

Vegan Mexican-Inspired Quinoa-Stuffed Bell Peppers: ..................................236

Vegan Mexican-Inspired Lentil Shepherd's Pie with Mashed Cauliflower: ......237

Vegan Mexican-Inspired Tempeh Fajitas with Smoky Paprika Sauce: .............238

Vegan Mexican-Inspired Chickpea and Spinach Enchiladas: ..........................239

Vegan Mexican-Inspired Ratatouille Tacos: ....................................................241

Vegan Mexican-Inspired Stuffed Artichokes with Roasted Red Pepper Sauce: 241

Vegan Mexican-Inspired Portobello Mushroom Steaks with Chimichurri: .......242

    Conclusion: ................................................................................................243

# INTRODUCTION

Welcome to a culinary journey that embraces the beauty and compassion of plant-based eating while honouring the diverse tapestry of Mexican cuisine. You are invited to go on a culinary trip with "Vibrant Flavors: A Vegan Journey Through Mexican Cuisine", that reimagines traditional Mexican meals using only plant-based components. This cookbook is your passport to a world of bright and healthy foods that celebrate tradition while embracing modern ethical choices, from the busy streets of Mexico City to the peaceful coastal communities. We bridge the gap between cultural authenticity and modern sustainability in this cookbook by providing a wide selection of delicious dishes that embody the spirit of Mexican cooking without compromising your principles. This collection of words will invigorate and enchant your taste buds whether you're a committed vegan, a curious flexitarian, or someone looking to include more plant-based meals in your diet. We'll delve into the core of Mexican culinary tradition chapter by chapter, highlighting the extraordinary variety of fruits, vegetables, grains, legumes, and spices. Each recipe is thoughtfully created to highlight the tastes that have made Mexican food so beloved worldwide. With a symphony of flavours and textures that will leave you craving more, "Vibrant Flavors" promises everything from hot street tacos to warming tamales, zesty salsas, and decadent sweets. Mexican food has long celebrated diversity, community, and culture. By adopting a plant-based diet, we respect this history and help create a more humane and sustainable world. Every ingredient and every meal represents the interdependence of all living things and the planet we call home, so keep that in mind as you set out on your culinary adventure. This cookbook is your guide to preparing delectable dishes that capture the spirit of Mexico, the energy of plants, and the joy of dining with loved ones, whether you're an experienced cook or a kitchen novice. So, prepare your knives and grab your apron as we set off on a pleasant tour of flavours that bridge cultures and bind people together. Prepare to be enchanted by

"Vibrant Flavors: A Vegan Journey Through Mexican Cuisine."
Your taste buds are about to go on an incredible journey.

## GUACAMOLE WITH PLANTAIN CHIPS:

***Ingredients:***

- 3 ripe avocados, peeled, pitted, and mashed
- 1 small red onion, finely chopped
- 2 cloves garlic, minced
- 1-2 jalapeno peppers, seeded and minced (adjust to taste)
- 1-2 limes, juiced
- 1/4 cup fresh cilantro, chopped
- Salt and pepper to taste
- Plantain chips for serving

***Instructions:***

1. Mix mashed avocados, chopped red onion, sliced garlic, jalapeno peppers, lime juice, and chopped cilantro.
2. Mix everything well and add salt and pepper to taste.
3. Plantain chips can be served with guacamole.

Nutrition (per serving):

- Calories: 180
- Fat: 14g
- Carbohydrates: 15g
- Fibre: 7g

- Protein: 2g

## SPICY SALSA VERDE WITH HOMEMADE TORTILLA CHIPS:

*Ingredients:*
- 1 lb tomatillos, husked and washed
- 2-3 serrano or jalapeno peppers (adjust to taste)
- 1 small onion, peeled and quartered
- 2 cloves garlic
- 1/4 cup fresh cilantro
- Salt to taste
- Corn tortillas, cut into triangles and baked or fried until crisp

*Instructions:*
1. To soften the tomatillos and peppers, boil them in a pot of water. Drain.
2. Cooked tomatillos, peppers, onion, garlic, cilantro, and salt are mixed in a mixer. Mix until it's smooth.
3. Serve the green salsa with the tortilla chips you made yourself.

*Nutrition (per serving):*
- Calories: 60
- Fat: 1g

- Carbohydrates: 14g
- Fibre: 3g
- Protein: 2g

## VEGAN QUESO FUNDIDO:

*Ingredients:*
- 1 cup raw cashews, soaked and drained
- 1 cup diced tomatoes
- 1/2 cup chopped bell peppers (assorted colours)
- 1/4 cup diced red onion
- 2 cloves garlic, minced
- 1 tablespoon nutritional yeast
- 1 teaspoon smoked paprika
- 1 teaspoon ground cumin
- Salt and pepper to taste
- Fresh cilantro for garnish
- Tortilla chips for serving

*Instructions:*
1. Blend cashews that have been soaked, diced tomatoes, chopped garlic, nutritional yeast, smoked paprika, cumin, salt, and pepper in a blender. Mix until it's smooth.
2. Diced bell peppers and red onion should be cooked in a pan until soft.

3. Pour the cashew mixture into the pan and cook it until it is warm and just a little bit thicker.
4. Serve with Mexican chips and fresh cilantro on top.

*Nutrition (per serving):*
- Calories: 180
- Fat: 11g
- Carbohydrates: 15g
- Fibre: 3g
- Protein: 7g

## STUFFED JALAPENO POPPERS:

*Ingredients:*
- 12 large jalapeno peppers, halved and seeded
- 1 cup vegan cream cheese
- 1/2 cup vegan cheddar cheese, shredded
- 1/4 cup diced red onion
- 2 cloves garlic, minced
- 1 teaspoon smoked paprika
- Salt and pepper to taste

*Instructions:*
1. Set the oven to 375°F (190°C) and put parchment paper on a baking sheet.

2. Vegan cream cheese, cheddar cheese, diced red onion, chopped garlic, smoked paprika, salt, and pepper are mixed in a bowl.
3. Stuff the cream cheese mixture into the jalapeno halves.
4. Put the stuffed jalapenos on the baking sheet and bake for 15 to 20 minutes until the filling is melted and bubbly.
5. The stuffed jalapeno poppers should be served hot.

*Nutrition (per serving):*
- Calories: 70
- Fat: 4g
- Carbohydrates: 7g
- Fiber: 2g
- Protein: 3g

## BLACK BEAN NACHOS:

*Ingredients:*
- 1 bag tortilla chips
- 1 can black beans, drained and rinsed
- 1 cup vegan cheddar cheese, shredded
- 1 cup diced tomatoes
- 1/2 cup diced red onion
- 1/4 cup chopped fresh cilantro
- 1-2 jalapeno peppers, sliced (adjust to taste)
- 1 avocado, diced

- Vegan sour cream for drizzling
- Sliced black olives for garnish

***Instructions:***
1. Set the oven to 375°F (190°C) and put parchment paper on a baking sheet.
2. Spread a single layer of chips on the baking sheet.
3. Sprinkle the chips with drained black beans and meatless cheddar cheese.
4. Bake for 10–15 minutes or until the cheese is bubbly and melting.
5. Remove from the oven and top with diced tomatoes, red onion, chopped cilantro, sliced jalapeno peppers, diced avocado, vegan sour cream, and sliced black olives.
6. The black bean nachos should be served right away.

***Nutrition (per serving):***
- Calories: 320
- Fat: 15g
- Carbohydrates: 38g
- Fibre: 6g
- Protein: 8g

## CORN AND AVOCADO SALSA:

***Ingredients:***

- 2 cups corn kernels (fresh, frozen, or canned)
- 2 ripe avocados, diced
- 1 cup diced tomatoes
- 1/2 cup diced red onion
- 1/4 cup chopped fresh cilantro
- Juice of 2 limes
- Salt and pepper to taste
- Optional: diced jalapeno for added heat

**Instructions:**
1. Mix corn kernels, diced avocado, diced tomatoes, diced red onion, chopped cilantro, and diced jalapeño (if using) in a bowl.
2. Pour lime juice over the mixture and toss it gently.
3. Salt and pepper can be added to taste.
4. Use your favourite tortilla chips to eat the corn and avocado salsa.

**Nutrition (per serving):**
- Calories: 160
- Fat: 9g
- Carbohydrates: 19g
- Fibre: 6g
  - Protein: 3g

## GRILLED STREET CORN WITH VEGAN CREMA:

*Ingredients:*
- 4 ears of corn, husked
- 1/4 cup vegan mayonnaise
- 2 tablespoons plain unsweetened vegan yoghurt
- Juice of 1 lime
- 1 teaspoon chilli powder
- Chopped fresh cilantro for garnish
- Lime wedges for serving

*Instructions:*
1. Set a grill or grill pan to medium-high heat to get it ready.
2. Turn the corn occasionally on the grill until it is browned and cooked all through, about 10 to 12 minutes.
3. Mix vegan mayonnaise, yoghurt, lime juice, and chilli powder in a bowl with a whisk to make the crema.
4. The vegan cream can be used to brush on the grilled corn.
5. Top the corn with chopped cilantro and serve with lime wedges.

*Nutrition (per serving):*
- Calories: 180

- Fat: 10g
- Carbohydrates: 24g
- Fibre: 3g
- Protein: 3g

## TOFU TAQUITOS WITH CHIPOTLE SAUCE:

*Ingredients:*
- 1 block extra-firm tofu, pressed and diced
- 1 tablespoon olive oil
- 1 teaspoon chilli powder
- 1/2 teaspoon ground cumin
- Salt and pepper to taste
- 8 small flour tortillas
- 1 cup shredded lettuce
- 1/2 cup diced tomatoes
- Chipotle Sauce: (Mix)
- 1/4 cup vegan mayonnaise
- 1 tablespoon adobo sauce (from canned chipotle peppers)
- Juice of 1 lime
- Salt to taste

*Instructions:*
1. Turn the oven on and set it to 375°F (190°C).
2. Mix chopped tofu with olive oil, chilli powder, cumin powder, salt, and pepper in a bowl.

3. Spread the tofu on a baking sheet and bake it for 20 to 25 minutes or until it gets crispy.
4. Warm the tortillas and put a spoonful of crispy tofu on each one.
5. Shred some cabbage and cut up some tomatoes to put on top.
6. To make taquitos, roll the tortillas up tight.
7. Put the chipotle sauce on the side with the tofu taquitos for dipping.

*Nutrition (per serving):*
- Calories: 220
- Fat: 12g
- Carbohydrates: 20g
- Fibre: 3g
- Protein: 8g

## VEGAN CEVICHE:

*Ingredients:*
- 1 cup hearts of palm, sliced
- 1 cup diced cucumber
- 1 cup diced tomatoes
- 1/2 cup diced red onion
- 1/4 cup chopped fresh cilantro
- Juice of 2 limes
- Juice of 1 lemon
- 2 tablespoons orange juice

- 2 tablespoons olive oil
- Salt and pepper to taste
- Optional: diced jalapeno for added heat

*Instructions:*
1. Mix hearts of palm, diced cucumber, tomatoes, red onion, chopped cilantro, and, if you're using it, diced jalapeño in a bowl.
2. Mix lime juice, lemon juice, orange juice, olive oil, salt, and pepper in a separate bowl with a whisk to make the marinade.
3. Pour the marinade over the vegetables and slowly mix it all.
4. Before serving, let the ceviche sit in the fridge for at least 30 minutes.
5. Put the veggie ceviche on tostadas or serve it with tortilla chips.

*Nutrition (per serving):*
- Calories: 150
- Fat: 8g
- Carbohydrates: 20g
- Fibre: 5g
- Protein: 3g

## ROASTED RED PEPPER AND WALNUT DIP:

*Ingredients:*
- 2 large red bell peppers, roasted, peeled, and seeded
- 1 cup walnuts, toasted
- 2 cloves garlic
- 2 tablespoons olive oil
- 1 tablespoon lemon juice
- 1 teaspoon ground cumin
- Salt and pepper to taste
- Optional: smoked paprika for garnish

*Instructions:*
1. Put roasted red bell peppers, toasted walnuts, garlic, olive oil, lemon juice, cumin powder, salt, and pepper into a food processor and blend.
2. Blend until smooth and creamy. If needed, add a splash of water to get the consistency you want.
3. If you want to use it, add smoked paprika on top of the dip before serving.
4. Serve the roasted red pepper and walnut dip with pita bread or fresh veggies.

*Nutrition (per serving):*
- Calories: 120
- Fat: 10g
- Carbohydrates: 5g
- Fiber: 2g
- Protein: 3g

## VEGAN TORTILLA SOUP:

*Ingredients:*
- 1 tablespoon olive oil
- 1 onion, chopped
- 3 cloves garlic, minced
- 1 bell pepper, chopped
- 1 carrot, diced
- 1 zucchini, diced
- 1 teaspoon ground cumin
- 1 teaspoon chilli powder
- 1/2 teaspoon smoked paprika
- 1 can (15 oz) diced tomatoes
- 6 cups vegetable broth
- 1 can (15 oz) black beans, drained and rinsed
- 1 cup corn kernels (fresh, frozen, or canned)
- Juice of 1 lime
- Salt and pepper to taste
- Tortilla strips, avocado, lime wedges, and chopped cilantro for garnish

*Instructions:*
1. Olive oil is heated over medium heat in a big pot. Cook the onion until it becomes clear.
2. Add chopped bell pepper, minced garlic, diced carrot, and sliced zucchini. Cook the veggies for a few minutes until they are soft.

3. Mix in the cumin, pepper powder, and smoked paprika that have been ground.
4. Add diced tomatoes and stock made from vegetables. Bring to a boil, boil the heat and let it cook for about 15 to 20 minutes.
5. Add the black beans and corn, then let it simmer for 10 more minutes.
6. Add lime juice and salt and pepper to taste.
7. Serve the soup hot with strips of tortilla, pieces of avocado, wedges of lime, and chopped cilantro on top.

***Nutrition (per serving):***
- Calories: 220
- Fat: 5g
- Carbohydrates: 38g
- Fibre: 10g
- Protein: 9g

## SPICY LENTIL POZOLE:

***Ingredients:***
- 1 cup dried brown or green lentils, rinsed and drained
- 1 onion, chopped
- 3 cloves garlic, minced
- 1 jalapeno pepper, seeded and minced
- 1 teaspoon ground cumin

- 1 teaspoon chilli powder
- 1/2 teaspoon smoked paprika
- 6 cups vegetable broth
- 1 can (15 oz) hominy, drained and rinsed
- 1 can (15 oz) diced tomatoes
- Juice of 1 lime
- Salt and pepper to taste
- Chopped fresh cilantro, sliced radishes, and lime wedges, for garnish

*Instructions:*

1. In a big pot, sauté chopped onion, minced garlic, and jalapeno pepper until the mixture smells good.
2. Add cumin, pepper powder, and smoked paprika that has been ground. Stir the onions to coat them.
3. Mix in lentils that have been washed, veggie broth, hominy, and diced tomatoes. Bring to a boil, turn down the heat and let it cook for about 20 to 25 minutes, or until the lentils are soft.
4. Add lime juice and salt and pepper to taste.
5. Serve the pozole hot, with chopped cilantro, thinly sliced radishes, and wedges of lime on top.

*Nutrition (per serving):*

- Calories: 220

- Fat: 1g
- Carbohydrates: 43g
- Fiber: 14g
- Protein: 12g

## CHIPOTLE BLACK BEAN SOUP:

*Ingredients:*
- 2 cans (15 oz each) of black beans, drained and rinsed
- 1 onion, chopped
- 3 cloves garlic, minced
- 1 chipotle pepper in adobo sauce, minced (adjust to taste)
- 1 teaspoon ground cumin
- 1 teaspoon dried oregano
- 4 cups vegetable broth
- 1 cup diced tomatoes
- Juice of 1 lime
- Salt and pepper to taste
- Optional toppings: vegan sour cream, chopped green onions, chopped cilantro

*Instructions:*
1. In a big pot, cook chopped onion and minced garlic until the onion and garlic are soft.

2. Add chopped chipotle pepper, ground cumin, and oregano that has been dried. Wait one more minute.
3. Add one can of black beans, one cup of veggie broth, and one cup of diced tomatoes. Use an immersion mixer to mix the mixture in parts until it is creamy.
4. Stir in the rest of the can of black beans and let it simmer for about 15 minutes.
5. Add lime juice and salt and pepper to taste.
6. Serve the soup hot, with toppings that you choose.

*Nutrition (per serving):*
- Calories: 190
- Fat: 1g
- Carbohydrates: 35g
- Fiber: 12g
- Protein: 11g

## CREAMY PUMPKIN AND CORN CHOWDER:

*Ingredients:*
 i. 1 tablespoon olive oil
 ii. 1 onion, chopped
 iii. 3 cloves garlic, minced
 iv. 2 cups diced potatoes

- v. 1 teaspoon ground cumin
- vi. 1/2 teaspoon ground coriander
- vii. 1/2 teaspoon smoked paprika
- viii. 2 cups vegetable broth
- ix. 1 can (15 oz) pumpkin puree
- x. 1 cup corn kernels (fresh, frozen, or canned)
- xi. 1 cup unsweetened coconut milk
- xii. Salt and pepper to taste
- xiii. Chopped fresh cilantro for garnish

**Instructions:**

1. Olive oil is heated over medium heat in a big pot. Cook the onion until it becomes clear.
2. Add chopped potatoes and sliced garlic. Cook for a short time.
3. Mix in the cumin, coriander, and smoked paprika that has been ground.
4. Add corn, veggie broth, and pumpkin puree. Bring to a boil, then turn down the heat and let it cook for about 15 to 20 minutes or until the potatoes are soft.
5. Add the coconut milk and let it warm up.
6. Add salt and pepper to taste.
7. The soup should be served hot with chopped cilantro on top.

**Nutrition (per serving):**

- Calories: 220

- Fat: 9g
- Carbohydrates: 33g
- Fibre: 6g
- Protein: 4g

## MEXICAN QUINOA CHILI:

*Ingredients:*
- 1 cup quinoa, rinsed and drained
- 1 onion, chopped
- 3 cloves garlic, minced
- 1 bell pepper, chopped
- 1 carrot, diced
- 1 zucchini, diced
- 1 teaspoon ground cumin
- 1 teaspoon chilli powder
- 1/2 teaspoon smoked paprika
- 1 can (15 oz) diced tomatoes
- 4 cups vegetable broth
- 1 can (15 oz) black beans, drained and rinsed
- 1 cup corn kernels (fresh, frozen, or canned)
- Juice of 1 lime
- Salt and pepper to taste
- Chopped fresh cilantro, diced avocado, and lime wedges for garnish

*Instructions:*

1. In a big pot, cook chopped onion in oil until it turns transparent.
2. Add chopped bell pepper, minced garlic, diced carrot, and sliced zucchini. Cook for a short time.
3. Mix in the cumin, pepper powder, and smoked paprika that have been ground.
4. Add diced tomatoes and stock made from vegetables. Bring to a boil, boil the heat and let it cook for about 15 to 20 minutes.
5. Add washed rice, corn, and black beans. Let it cook for 15 minutes or until the quinoa is done and the veggies are soft.
6. Add lime juice and salt and pepper to taste.
7. Serve the hot quinoa soup, with cilantro, avocado, and lime wedges.

*Nutrition (per serving):*
- Calories: 240
- Fat: 4g
- Carbohydrates: 43g
- Fiber: 9g
- Protein: 10g

## ROASTED TOMATO AND RED PEPPER GAZPACHO:

*Ingredients:*

- 4 large tomatoes, roasted and peeled
- 2 red bell peppers, roasted and peeled
- 1 cucumber, peeled and chopped
- 1 small red onion, chopped
- 2 cloves garlic, minced
- 2 tablespoons olive oil
- 2 tablespoons red wine vinegar
- 2 cups vegetable broth
- Salt and pepper to taste
- Chopped fresh basil for garnish
- Optional: croutons for serving

*Instructions:*
1. Put roasted tomatoes, red bell peppers, chopped cucumber, chopped red onion, minced garlic, olive oil, red wine vinegar, and vegetable broth in a blender and blend until smooth.
2. Mix until it's smooth. If the gazpacho is too thick, you can thin it out by adding more water or veggie broth.
3. Salt and pepper can be added to taste.
4. Before you serve the gazpacho, put it in the fridge for at least an hour.
5. Serve the cold gazpacho with chopped basil and, if you want, croutons on top.

*Nutrition (per serving):*

- Calories: 100
- Fat: 6g
- Carbohydrates: 12g
- Fibre: 3g
- Protein: 2g

## SOPA DE FIDEOS (VEGAN MEXICAN NOODLE SOUP):

*Ingredients:*
- 2 tablespoons olive oil
- 1 cup fideo noodles (or thin spaghetti, broken into pieces)
- 1 onion, chopped
- 3 cloves garlic, minced
- 1 teaspoon ground cumin
- 1/2 teaspoon smoked paprika
- 6 cups vegetable broth
- 1 can (15 oz) diced tomatoes
- Juice of 1 lime
- Salt and pepper to taste
- Chopped fresh cilantro, sliced green onions, and lime wedges for garnish

*Instructions:*
1. Olive oil is heated over medium heat in a big pot. Toast the fideo noodles until they are golden brown.

2. Cook the onion until it becomes clear.
3. Add chopped garlic, cumin powder, and smoked paprika. Wait one more minute.
4. Add tomato chunks and veggie broth. Bring to a boil, boil the heat and let it cook for about 15 to 20 minutes.
5. Add lime juice and salt and pepper to taste.
6. Serve the Sopa de fideos hot, with chopped cilantro, thinly sliced green onions, and wedges of lime on top.

*Nutrition (per serving):*
- Calories: 180
- Fat: 6g
- Carbohydrates: 27g
- Fibre: 3g
- Protein: 4g

## THREE-BEAN VEGAN CHILI:

*Ingredients:*
- 1 tablespoon olive oil
- 1 onion, chopped
- 3 cloves garlic, minced
- 1 bell pepper, chopped
- 1 carrot, diced
- 1 zucchini, diced
- 1 teaspoon ground cumin

- 1 teaspoon chilli powder
- 1/2 teaspoon smoked paprika
- 1 can (15 oz) diced tomatoes
- 1 can (15 oz) kidney beans, drained and rinsed
- 1 can (15 oz) black beans, drained and rinsed
- 1 can (15 oz) pinto beans, drained and rinsed
- 2 cups vegetable broth
- Salt and pepper to taste
- Chopped fresh cilantro, chopped green onions, and vegan shredded cheese for garnish

**Instructions:**
1. Olive oil is heated over medium heat in a big pot. Cook the onion until it becomes clear.
2. Add chopped bell pepper, minced garlic, diced carrot, and sliced zucchini. Cook for a short time.
3. Mix in the cumin, pepper powder, and smoked paprika that have been ground.
4. Add chopped tomatoes, kidney beans, black beans, pinto beans, and veggie broth. Bring to a boil, boil the heat and let it cook for about 20–25 minutes.
5. Salt and pepper can be added to taste.

6. The three-bean soup should be served hot and topped with chopped cilantro, green onions, and shredded vegan cheese.

*Nutrition (per serving):*
- Calories: 240
- Fat: 2g
- Carbohydrates: 44g
- Fiber: 14g
- Protein: 14g

## CALABACITAS SOUP:

*Ingredients:*
- 2 tablespoons olive oil
- 1 onion, chopped
- 3 cloves garlic, minced
- 2 zucchinis, diced
- 1 yellow squash, diced
- 1 can (15 oz) diced tomatoes
- 4 cups vegetable broth
- 1 teaspoon ground cumin
- 1/2 teaspoon chilli powder
- Salt and pepper to taste
- Chopped fresh cilantro for garnish

*Instructions:*
1. Olive oil is heated over medium heat in a big pot. Cook the onion until it becomes clear.

2. Add minced garlic, diced yellow squash, and sliced zucchini. Cook for a short time.
3. Mix in diced tomatoes, veggie broth, chilli powder, and ground cumin. Bring to a boil, boil the heat and let it cook for about 15 to 20 minutes.
4. Salt and pepper can be added to taste.
5. The calabacitas soup should be served hot and topped with chopped cilantro.

*Nutrition (per serving):*
- Calories: 120
- Fat: 6g
- Carbohydrates: 16g
- Fibre: 4g
- Protein: 3g

## POZOLE VERDE WITH JACKFRUIT:

*Ingredients:*
- 2 cans (20 oz each) of young jackfruit in brine, drained and rinsed
- 1 onion, chopped
- 3 cloves garlic, minced
- 1 can (15 oz) hominy, drained and rinsed
- 1 can (4 oz) diced green chillies
- 4 cups vegetable broth
- 1 teaspoon ground cumin

- 1/2 teaspoon dried oregano
- Salt and pepper to taste
- Toppings: sliced radishes, chopped fresh cilantro, diced avocado, lime wedges

***Instructions:***
1. In a big pot, cook chopped onion in oil until it turns transparent.
2. Add the minced garlic and cook for another minute.
3. Add the jackfruit that has been rinsed and drained, along with the hominy, diced green chillies, veggie broth, ground cumin, and dried oregano. Bring to a boil, then turn down the heat and let it cook for about 20–25 minutes.
4. Shred the jackfruit into small pieces with a fork.
5. Salt and pepper can be added to taste.
6. Serve the green pozole hot, with sliced radishes, chopped cilantro, diced avocado, and wedges of lime on top.

***Nutrition (per serving):***
- Calories: 180
- Fat: 2g
- Carbohydrates: 36g
- Fibre: 6g
- Protein: 6g

## VEGAN TACOS AL PASTOR:

*Ingredients for Tofu Marinade:*

- 1 block extra-firm tofu, pressed and sliced
- 1/4 cup pineapple juice
- 2 tablespoons achiote paste
- 2 tablespoons lime juice
- 1 tablespoon soy sauce
- 1 teaspoon ground cumin
- 1 teaspoon smoked paprika
- 1/2 teaspoon oregano
- Salt and pepper to taste

**For Tacos:**

- Corn tortillas
- Sliced pineapple
- Chopped onion and cilantro for garnish

*Instructions:*

1. Mix all of the ingredients for the sauce in a bowl.
2. Marinate slices of tofu for at least half an hour.
3. Cook the tofu on a grill or pan until golden and slightly crispy.
4. Warm up corn tortillas and put cooked tofu, sliced pineapple, chopped onion, and chopped cilantro on them to make tacos.

*Nutrition (per serving - 2 tacos):*
- Calories: 220
- Fat: 8g
- Carbohydrates: 26g
- Fibre: 4g
- Protein: 14g

## MUSHROOM AND SPINACH ENCHILADAS:

**Ingredients:**
- 8 small flour tortillas
- 2 cups sliced mushrooms
- 2 cups fresh spinach
- 1 onion, chopped
- 3 cloves garlic, minced
- 1 teaspoon ground cumin
- 1/2 teaspoon chilli powder
- 1/2 teaspoon dried oregano
- 2 cups vegan enchilada sauce
- 1 cup vegan shredded cheese
- Chopped fresh cilantro for garnish

**Instructions:**
1. Turn the oven on and set it to 375°F (190°C).
2. In a pan, cook chopped onion until it turns transparent.

3. Add chopped garlic, sliced mushrooms, ground cumin, chilli powder, and dried oregano. Cook the mushrooms until they are soft.
4. Cook the spinach until it wilts. Take off the heat.
5. Warm up the tortillas and put the mushroom and spinach filling in each one.
6. Roll it up and put it in an oven-safe dish.
7. Pour enchilada sauce over the tortillas that have been rolled, and then sprinkle vegan shredded cheese on top.
8. Bake for 15 to 20 minutes or until the cheese is bubbly and melted.
9. Before serving, sprinkle chopped cilantro on top.

*Nutrition (per serving - 2 enchiladas):*
- Calories: 320
- Fat: 15g
- Carbohydrates: 35g
- Fiber: 6g
- Protein: 10g

## CAULIFLOWER TINGA TOSTADAS:

*Ingredients:*
- 1 small head cauliflower, cut into florets
- 1 onion, chopped

- 3 cloves garlic, minced
- 1 can (15 oz) diced tomatoes
- 2 chipotle peppers in adobo sauce, minced
- 1 teaspoon dried oregano
- 1 teaspoon smoked paprika
- Salt and pepper to taste
- Tostada shells
- Sliced avocado, chopped onion, and chopped cilantro for garnish

*Instructions:*
1. In a big pan, cook the chopped onion until it turns transparent.
2. Add chopped garlic, diced tomatoes, chipotle peppers, dried oregano, and smoked paprika. Cook for a short time.
3. Add the pieces of cauliflower and cook until they are soft.
4. Lightly mash the cauliflower with a fork and mix it with the sauce.
5. Add salt and pepper to taste.
6. Warm up the tostada shells and put cauliflower tinga, avocado slices, chopped onion, and cilantro on them.

*Nutrition (per serving - 2 tostadas):*
- Calories: 220
- Fat: 8g

- Carbohydrates: 34g
- Fiber: 8g
- Protein: 6g

## VEGAN CHILES RELLENOS:

*Ingredients:*
- 4 large poblano peppers
- 1 cup cooked quinoa or rice
- 1 cup black beans, drained and rinsed
- 1 cup corn kernels (fresh, frozen, or canned)
- 1 cup vegan shredded cheese
- 2 cups tomato sauce
- 1 teaspoon ground cumin
- 1/2 teaspoon chilli powder
- Salt and pepper to taste
- Chopped fresh cilantro for garnish

*Instructions:*
1. Turn the oven on and set it to 375°F (190°C).
2. Char poblano peppers by roasting them. Put in a sealed plastic bag to steam, peel, remove the seeds, and set away.
3. Mix cooked quinoa or rice, black beans, corn, and chopped vegan cheese in a bowl.
4. Stuff the rice and bean mix into each poblano pepper.

5. Put peppers that have been stuffed in a baking dish.
6. Mix the tomato sauce, ground cumin, chilli powder, salt, and pepper in a separate bowl.
7. Pour the tomato sauce mix over the peppers that have been stuffed.
8. Bake for about 15 to 20 minutes or until everything is hot.
9. Before serving, sprinkle chopped cilantro on top.

*Nutrition (per serving - 1 stuffed pepper):*
- Calories: 280
- Fat: 8g
- Carbohydrates: 40g
- Fibre: 8g
- Protein: 12g

## JACKFRUIT CARNITAS BURRITOS:

*Ingredients:*
- 2 cans (20 oz each) of young jackfruit in brine, drained and rinsed
- 1 onion, chopped
- 3 cloves garlic, minced
- 1 teaspoon ground cumin
- 1 teaspoon chilli powder
- 1/2 teaspoon smoked paprika

- 1/2 teaspoon dried oregano
- Salt and pepper to taste
- Flour tortillas
- Mexican rice
- Black beans drained and rinsed
- Sliced avocado, diced tomatoes, and chopped cilantro, for garnish

**Instructions:**
1. In a pan, cook chopped onion until it turns transparent.
2. Add chopped garlic and jackfruit that has been drained. Cook for a short time.
3. Shred the jackfruit into small pieces with a fork.
4. Mix in the ground cumin, chilli powder, smoked paprika, dried oregano, salt, and pepper.
5. Warm flour tortillas and put jackfruit carnitas, Mexican rice, black beans, avocado slices, diced tomatoes, and chopped cilantro in them to make burritos.

**Nutrition (per serving - 1 burrito):**
- Calories: 340
- Fat: 6g
- Carbohydrates: 60g
- Fibre: 10g
- Protein: 10g

## VEGAN MOLE POBLANO:

*Ingredients:*

- 2 dried ancho chillies, stemmed and seeded
- 2 dried guajillo chillies, stemmed and seeded
- 1 onion, chopped
- 3 cloves garlic, minced
- 1/2 cup tomato sauce
- 1/4 cup peanut butter
- 1/4 cup unsweetened cocoa powder
- 1 teaspoon ground cumin
- 1/2 teaspoon ground cinnamon
- 1/4 teaspoon ground cloves
- 2 cups vegetable broth
- Salt and pepper to taste
- Sliced cooked potatoes or tortillas for serving

*Instructions:*

1. Toast dried chillies in a dry pan until they smell good. Take it out and soak it for about 15 minutes in hot water. Drain and put away.
2. In the same pan, cook the chopped onion until it becomes clear.
3. Add the chopped garlic, tomato sauce, peanut butter, cocoa powder, cumin, cinnamon, and cloves that have been ground. Cook for a short time.

4. Mix the onion and spices with the chillies soaked in veggie broth until smooth.
5. Put the sauce back in the pan and boil until it thickens.
6. Add salt and pepper to taste.
7. Serve the mole poblano overcooked tortillas or sliced potatoes.

*Nutrition (per serving - mole sauce only):*
- Calories: 80
- Fat: 5g
- Carbohydrates: 9g
- Fibre: 3g
- Protein: 3g

## TOFU AND VEGETABLE FAJITAS:

*Ingredients:*
- 1 block extra-firm tofu, pressed and sliced
- 1 onion, sliced
- 1 bell pepper, sliced
- 1 zucchini, sliced
- 1 teaspoon ground cumin
- 1 teaspoon chilli powder
- 1/2 teaspoon smoked paprika
- Juice of 1 lime
- Salt and pepper to taste
- Flour tortillas

- Sliced avocado, vegan sour cream, and chopped cilantro for garnish

*Instructions:*
1. In a pan, cook sliced onion until it turns transparent.
2. Add bell pepper and zucchini cut into thin slices. Cook the veggies until they are soft.
3. Move the veggies to one side of the pan and add the tofu slices. Cook the tofu until it turns gold.
4. Mix in the ground cumin, chilli powder, smoked paprika, lime juice, salt, and pepper.
5. Warm flour tortillas and put the tofu and vegetables in them to make fajitas.
6. Add slices of avocado, chopped cilantro, and vegan sour cream to the top.

*Nutrition (per serving - 2 fajitas):*
- Calories: 280
- Fat: 12g
- Carbohydrates: 32g
- Fiber: 7g
- Protein: 14g

## VEGAN TAMALES WITH SALSA ROJA:

*Ingredients for Tamales:*
- 2 cups masa harina

- 1 teaspoon baking powder
- 1 teaspoon ground cumin
- 1/2 teaspoon chilli powder
- 1/2 teaspoon salt
- 1/2 cup vegetable oil
- 1 1/2 cups vegetable broth
- Corn husks soaked in warm water

**For Filling:**

- 1 cup cooked black beans
- 1 cup cooked Mexican rice
- Salsa Roja

*Instructions:*
1. Mix the masa harina, baking powder, cumin powder, chilli powder, and salt in a bowl.
2. Gradually add veggie oil and broth, and mix until a dough forms.
3. Spread wet corn husks with masa dough.
4. Put a spoonful of cooked black beans and Mexican rice in the middle of each tamale.
5. Roll the tamales up and tie them with strips of wet corn husk.
6. Tamales should be steamed for 45–60 minutes or until hard-cooked.
7. Serve red salsa with tamales.

*Nutrition (per serving - 2 tamales):*

- Calories: 320
- Fat: 12g
- Carbohydrates: 48g
- Fibre: 6g
- Protein: 8g

## POTATO AND POBLANO FLAUTAS:

***Ingredients:***
- Four large flour tortillas
- 2 cups cooked and mashed potatoes
- 2 poblano peppers, roasted, peeled, and chopped
- 1 onion, chopped
- 3 cloves garlic, minced
- 1 teaspoon ground cumin
- 1/2 teaspoon chilli powder
- Salt and pepper to taste
- Cooking spray or oil for brushing

***Instructions:***
1. In a pan, cook chopped onion until it turns transparent.
2. Add chopped roasted poblano peppers, sliced garlic, ground cumin, and chilli powder. Cook for a short time.
3. Mix in mashed cooked potatoes. Add salt and pepper to taste.

4. Warm up some flour tortillas and spoon the potato filling on each one.
5. To make flautas, roll the tortillas up tight.
6. Use food spray or oil to brush the flautas.
7. Bake at 375°F (190°C) in an oven warmed for 15 to 20 minutes until crisp and golden.
8. Serve flautas with salsa or any other sauce you like.

*Nutrition (per serving - 2 flautas):*
- Calories: 280
- Fat: 8g
- Carbohydrates: 45g
- Fiber: 6g
- Protein: 6g

## STUFFED BELL PEPPERS WITH MEXICAN RICE AND BLACK BEANS:

*Ingredients:*
- Four large bell peppers, tops removed and seeded
- 2 cups cooked Mexican rice
- 1 cup black beans, drained and rinsed
- 1 cup diced tomatoes
- 1/2 cup corn kernels (fresh, frozen, or canned)
- 1 teaspoon ground cumin

- 1/2 teaspoon chilli powder
- Salt and pepper to taste
- Vegan shredded cheese for topping

*Instructions:*
1. Turn the oven on and set it to 375°F (190°C).
2. Cooked Mexican rice, black beans, chopped tomatoes, corn kernels, cumin powder, and chilli powder are mixed in a bowl.
3. Add salt and pepper to taste.
4. Stuff the rice and beans into each bell pepper.
5. Put bell peppers stuffed in a baking dish and sprinkle vegan shredded cheese on top.
6. Bake for 20 to 25 minutes or until the peppers are soft and the cheese is melted.
7. Serve bell peppers with hot stuffing.

*Nutrition (per serving - 1 stuffed pepper):*
- Calories: 260
- Fat: 4g
- Carbohydrates: 48g
- Fibre: 8g
- Protein: 9g

## MEXICAN RICE WITH CHARRED CORN:

*Ingredients:*

- 1 cup long-grain white rice
- 2 cups vegetable broth
- 1 cup corn kernels (fresh, frozen, or canned)
- 1 tablespoon olive oil
- 1 onion, chopped
- 3 cloves garlic, minced
- 1 teaspoon ground cumin
- 1/2 teaspoon chilli powder
- Salt and pepper to taste
- Chopped fresh cilantro for garnish

**Instructions:**
1. Olive oil is heated in a pot over medium heat. Cook the onion until it becomes clear.
2. Mix in chopped garlic, cumin powder, and chilli powder. Wait one more minute.
3. Add the rice and cook it for a few minutes until it gets a light toast.
4. Stir in the veggie broth and bring to a boil. Turn down the heat, cover it, and let it cook slowly until the rice is done.
5. In a different pan, char corn kernels until they get a bit black.
6. Mix the burned corn into the cooked rice in a gentle way.
7. Add salt and pepper to taste.
8. Before serving, sprinkle chopped cilantro on top.

*Nutrition (per serving):*
- Calories: 200
- Fat: 2g
- Carbohydrates: 42g
- Fiber: 2g
- Protein: 4g

## SPICY BLACK BEANS WITH CILANTRO LIME RICE:

*Ingredients for Black Beans:*
- 2 cans (15 oz each) of black beans, drained and rinsed
- 1 onion, chopped
- 3 cloves garlic, minced
- 1 jalapeno pepper, minced
- 1 teaspoon ground cumin
- 1/2 teaspoon chilli powder
- Juice of 1 lime
- Salt and pepper to taste

**For Cilantro Lime Rice:**

- 1 cup long-grain white rice
- 2 cups vegetable broth
- Juice of 1 lime
- Chopped fresh cilantro for garnish

***Instructions:***
1. In a pan, cook chopped onion until it turns transparent.
2. Add chopped garlic and chopped jalapeno. Wait one more minute.
3. Add cumin and pepper powder that has been ground.
4. Cook the black beans until they are warm.
5. Mix in salt, pepper, and lime juice.
6. In a different pot, mix rice and veggie broth. Bring to a boil, turn down the heat, put a lid on it, and let it simmer until the rice is done.
7. Mix chopped cilantro and lime juice into the cooked rice.
8. Serve cilantro lime rice with hot black beans.

***Nutrition (per serving - beans and rice):***
- Calories: 320
- Fat: 1g
- Carbohydrates: 66g
- Fiber: 10g
- Protein: 13g

## VEGAN REFRIED BEANS:

***Ingredients:***
- 2 cans (15 oz each) of pinto beans, drained and rinsed

- 1 onion, chopped
- 3 cloves garlic, minced
- 1 teaspoon ground cumin
- 1/2 teaspoon chilli powder
- Salt and pepper to taste
- Chopped fresh cilantro for garnish

***Instructions:***
1. In a pan, cook chopped onion until it turns transparent.
2. Add the minced garlic and cook for another minute.
3. Add cumin and pepper powder that has been ground.
4. Please put in the pinto beans and cook until they are warm.
5. To get the desired texture, you can mash the beans with a potato masher or a fork.
6. Add salt and pepper to taste.
7. Before serving, sprinkle chopped cilantro on top.

***Nutrition (per serving):***
- Calories: 180
- Fat: 1g
- Carbohydrates: 33g
- Fiber: 9g
- Protein: 10g

## CHIPOTLE LIME QUINOA:

*Ingredients:*
- 1 cup quinoa, rinsed and drained
- 2 cups vegetable broth
- 2 chipotle peppers in adobo sauce, minced
- Juice of 1 lime
- Chopped fresh cilantro for garnish

*Instructions:*
1. Mix quinoa and veggie broth in a pot. Bring to a boil, turn down the heat, cover, and let it simmer until the quinoa is done.
2. Add chopped chipotle peppers and lime juice and mix well.
3. Before serving, sprinkle chopped cilantro on top.

*Nutrition (per serving):*
- Calories: 220
- Fat: 3g
- Carbohydrates: 39g
- Fibre: 4g
- Protein: 6g

## CUMIN-SCENTED BROWN RICE:

*Ingredients:*

- 1 cup brown rice
- 2 cups vegetable broth
- 1 teaspoon ground cumin
- Juice of 1 lime
- Chopped fresh cilantro for garnish

*Instructions:*
1. Mix brown rice and veggie broth in a saucepan. Bring to a boil, turn down the heat, put a lid on it, and let it simmer until the rice is done.
2. Mix in the cumin powder and lime juice.
3. Before serving, sprinkle chopped cilantro on top.

*Nutrition (per serving):*
- Calories: 200
- Fat: 1g
- Carbohydrates: 44g
- Fibre: 4g
- Protein: 4g

## COCONUT CILANTRO LIME RICE:

*Ingredients:*
- 1 cup long-grain white rice
- 1 cup canned coconut milk
- 1 cup water
- Juice of 1 lime
- Chopped fresh cilantro for garnish

*Instructions:*
1. Mix rice, coconut milk, and water in a pot. Bring to a boil, turn down the heat, put a lid on it, and let it simmer until the rice is done.
2. Add lime juice and stir.
3. Before serving, sprinkle chopped cilantro on top.

*Nutrition (per serving):*
- Calories: 240
- Fat: 9g
- Carbohydrates: 36g
- Fibre: 1g
- Protein: 4g

## PINTO BEAN AND RICE BURRITO BOWL:

*Ingredients:*
- 1 cup cooked pinto beans
- 1 cup cooked white or brown rice
- 1 bell pepper, chopped
- 1 tomato, diced
- 1/2 red onion, chopped
- 1/4 cup chopped fresh cilantro
- Juice of 1 lime
- Salt and pepper to taste
- Sliced avocado for garnish

*Instructions:*
1. Cooked pinto beans, cooked rice, chopped bell pepper, diced tomato, chopped red onion, chopped cilantro, and lime juice are all mixed in a bowl.
2. Add salt and pepper to taste.
3. Slice an avocado and put it on top of the burrito bowl.

*Nutrition (per serving):*
- Calories: 320
- Fat: 2g
- Carbohydrates: 64g
- Fiber: 12g
- Protein: 12g

## RED RICE WITH ROASTED PEPPERS:

*Ingredients:*
- 1 cup long-grain white rice
- 2 cups vegetable broth
- 1 red bell pepper, roasted, peeled, and chopped
- 1/2 red onion, chopped
- 2 cloves garlic, minced
- 1 teaspoon ground cumin

- 1/2 teaspoon chilli powder
- Juice of 1 lime
- Chopped fresh cilantro for garnish

*Instructions:*
1. Mix rice and veggie broth in a pot. Bring to a boil, turn down the heat, put a lid on it, and let it simmer until the rice is done.
2. In a pan, cook the chopped red onion until it turns transparent.
3. Mix in chopped garlic, cumin powder, and chilli powder. Wait one more minute.
4. Cook for a few minutes after adding the roasted red bell pepper.
5. Mix the roasted pepper mixture with the cooked rice in a gentle way.
6. Add lime juice to taste and sprinkle chopped cilantro on top before serving.

*Nutrition (per serving):*
- Calories: 220
- Fat: 1g
- Carbohydrates: 46g
- Fiber: 2g
- Protein: 4g

## VEGAN BLACK BEAN AND CORN SALAD:

*Ingredients:*
- 2 cans (15 oz each) of black beans, drained and rinsed
- 1 cup corn kernels (fresh, frozen, or canned)
- 1 red bell pepper, diced
- 1/2 red onion, chopped
- 1 jalapeno pepper, minced
- Juice of 2 limes
- 2 tablespoons chopped fresh cilantro
- Salt and pepper to taste

*Instructions:*
1. Mix black beans, corn kernels, diced red bell pepper, chopped red onion, minced jalapeno pepper, lime juice, and chopped cilantro in a bowl.
2. Add salt and pepper to taste.
3. The black bean and corn salad should be served cold.

*Nutrition (per serving):*
- Calories: 240
- Fat: 1g
- Carbohydrates: 48g
- Fiber: 15g
- Protein: 14g

## THREE-BEAN QUINOA SALAD:

*Ingredients:*
- 1 cup cooked quinoa
- 1 can (15 oz) black beans, drained and rinsed
- 1 can (15 oz) kidney beans, drained and rinsed
- 1 can (15 oz) chickpeas, drained and rinsed
- 1 bell pepper, chopped
- 1/2 red onion, chopped
- 1/4 cup chopped fresh parsley
- Juice of 2 lemons
- 2 tablespoons olive oil
- Salt and pepper to taste

*Instructions:*
1. Mix cooked quinoa, black beans, kidney beans, chickpeas, chopped red onion, bell pepper, and parsley in a big bowl.
2. Mix lemon juice, olive oil, salt, and pepper in a different bowl with a whisk to make the dressing.
3. The dressing goes on top of the rice and beans.
4. Toss them together well.
5. The three-bean quinoa salad should be served cold.

*Nutrition (per serving):*
- Calories: 320
- Fat: 8g

- Carbohydrates: 50g
- Fiber: 12g
- Protein: 15g

## GRILLED CACTUS SALAD:

*Ingredients:*
- 2 cactus paddles (nopales), cleaned and sliced
- 1 tablespoon olive oil
- Salt and pepper to taste
- 1 tomato, diced
- 1/2 red onion, chopped
- 1 jalapeno pepper, minced
- Juice of 1 lime
- Chopped fresh cilantro for garnish

*Instructions:*
1. Salt and pepper the cactus slices after brushing them with olive oil.
2. Grill slices of cactus until they are soft and a little bit blackened.
3. Mix cooked cactus, diced tomato, chopped red onion, minced jalapeno pepper, and lime juice in a bowl.
4. Add salt and pepper to taste.

5. Before serving, sprinkle chopped cilantro on top.

**Nutrition (per serving):**
- Calories: 60
- Fat: 3g
- Carbohydrates: 8g
- Fibre: 3g
- Protein: 1g

## JICAMA AND MANGO SLAW:

**Ingredients:**
- 1 jicama, peeled and julienned
- 1 ripe mango, peeled and julienned
- 1/2 red onion, thinly sliced
- Juice of 2 limes
- 2 tablespoons chopped fresh cilantro
- Salt and pepper to taste

**Instructions:**
1. Mix jicama, mango, thinly sliced red onion, lime juice, and chopped cilantro in a bowl.
2. Season with salt and pepper.
3. Toss well to combine.
4. Serve the jicama and mango slaw cold.

**Nutrition (per serving):**
- Calories: 70
- Fat: 0.5g

- Carbohydrates: 18g
- Fibre: 6g
- Protein: 1g

## ROASTED SWEET POTATO AND AVOCADO SALAD:

***Ingredients:***
- 2 medium sweet potatoes, peeled and cubed
- 1 tablespoon olive oil
- Salt and pepper to taste
- 2 avocados, diced
- 1 red onion, thinly sliced
- Juice of 2 limes
- 2 tablespoons chopped fresh cilantro

***Instructions:***
1. Turn the oven on and set it to 400°F (200°C).
2. Mix cubes of sweet potato, olive oil, salt, and pepper.
3. Roast sweet potatoes in the oven until they are soft and browned.
4. Mix baked sweet potatoes, diced avocado, thinly sliced red onion, lime juice, and chopped cilantro.
5. Toss them together well.

6. The sweet potato and avocado salad can be served warm or at room temperature.

*Nutrition (per serving):*
- Calories: 220
- Fat: 10g
- Carbohydrates: 32g
- Fibre: 8g
- Protein: 3g

## MEXICAN STREET CORN SALAD:

*Ingredients:*
- 4 cups cooked corn kernels (fresh, frozen, or canned)
- 1/2 cup vegan mayonnaise
- 1/4 cup chopped fresh cilantro
- 1/4 cup vegan cotija cheese or nutritional yeast
- 1 teaspoon chilli powder
- Juice of 1 lime
- Salt and pepper to taste

*Instructions:*
1. Mix cooked corn kernels, vegan mayonnaise, chopped cilantro, vegan cotija cheese or nutritional yeast, chilli powder, and lime juice in a bowl.
2. Add salt and pepper to taste.

3. Toss them together well.
4. The street corn salad should be served cold.

*Nutrition (per serving):*
- Calories: 180
- Fat: 10g
- Carbohydrates: 23g
- Fibre: 3g
- Protein: 3g

## VEGAN CAESAR SALAD WITH PEPITAS:

*Ingredients for Dressing:*
- 1/2 cup raw cashews, soaked and drained
- 1/4 cup water
- 2 tablespoons lemon juice
- 1 tablespoon nutritional yeast
- 1 clove garlic, minced
- 1 teaspoon Dijon mustard
- Salt and pepper to taste

**For Salad:**

- Romaine lettuce, chopped
- Croutons (vegan if desired)
- Roasted pepitas (pumpkin seeds)
- Lemon wedges

*Instructions:*
1. Soaked cashews, water, lemon juice, nutritional yeast, chopped garlic, Dijon mustard, salt, and pepper are blended until smooth.
2. Mix the Caesar dressing with the chopped romaine leaves in a large bowl.
3. Add croutons and spiced pepitas to the top.
4. Lemon wedges should be put on top of the veggie Caesar salad.

*Nutrition (per serving - salad and dressing):*
- Calories: 220
- Fat: 14g
- Carbohydrates: 19g
- Fibre: 6g
- Protein: 8g

## TOMATO AND AVOCADO SALAD WITH LIME DRESSING:

*Ingredients:*
- 4 large tomatoes, diced
- 2 avocados, diced
- 1/2 red onion, thinly sliced
- Juice of 2 limes
- 2 tablespoons chopped fresh cilantro
- Salt and pepper to taste

*Instructions:*

1. Mix chopped tomatoes, chopped avocado, thinly sliced red onion, chopped cilantro, and lime juice in a bowl.
2. Add salt and pepper to taste.
3. Toss them together well.
4. The tomato and avocado salad should be served cold.

*Nutrition (per serving):*
- Calories: 180
- Fat: 15g
- Carbohydrates: 12g
- Fibre: 7g
- Protein: 3g

## CHARRED ZUCCHINI WITH CILANTRO AND LIME:

*Ingredients:*
- 4 medium zucchini, sliced lengthwise
- 1 tablespoon olive oil
- Salt and pepper to taste
- Juice of 1 lime
- Chopped fresh cilantro for garnish

*Instructions:*
1. Salt and pepper the zucchini slices after brushing them with olive oil.

2. Slice zucchini and grill it or cook it in a pan until it is browned and soft.
3. Pour lime juice on top and sprinkle chopped cilantro on top before serving.

*Nutrition (per serving):*
- Calories: 40
- Fat: 3g
- Carbohydrates: 4g
- Fibre: 1g
- Protein: 1g

## ROASTED BEET AND ORANGE SALAD:

**Ingredients:**
- 4 medium beets, roasted, peeled, and sliced
- 2 oranges, peeled and segmented
- 1/4 red onion, thinly sliced
- 2 tablespoons chopped fresh mint
- Juice of 1 lemon
- 1 tablespoon olive oil
- Salt and pepper to taste

**Instructions:**
1. Slices of roasted beet, orange segments, thinly sliced red onion, chopped mint, lemon juice, and olive oil are all mixed in a bowl.

2. Add salt and pepper to taste.
3. Toss them together well.
4. The beet and orange salad should be served cold.

*Nutrition (per serving):*
- Calories: 120
- Fat: 3g
- Carbohydrates: 23g
- Fibre: 5g
- Protein: 3g

## SPICY PICKLED RED ONIONS:

*Ingredients:*
- 1 large red onion, thinly sliced
- 1/2 cup apple cider vinegar
- 1/4 cup water
- 2 tablespoons maple syrup or agave nectar
- 1 teaspoon red pepper flakes
- 1 teaspoon whole black peppercorns
- 1 teaspoon salt

*Instructions:*
1. Mix salt, red pepper flakes, black peppercorns, apple cider vinegar, maple syrup or agave nectar, and maple syrup or agave nectar in a pot.

2. Bring the mixture to a boil, remove it from the heat and let it cool down slightly.
3. Slice the red onion very thinly and put it in a glass jar.
4. Pour the juice used to pickle the onions over them.
5. Close the lid and put the jar in the fridge for at least an hour before you use it.
6. Serve the tangy and spicy pickled red onions as a dressing.

*Nutrition (per serving - 2 tablespoons):*
- Calories: 20
- Fat: 0g
- Carbohydrates: 5g
- Fibre: 1g
- Protein: 0g

## QUINOA AND BLACK BEAN STUFFED BELL PEPPERS:

*Ingredients:*
- 4 large bell peppers, tops removed and seeded
- 1 cup cooked quinoa
- 1 cup cooked black beans
- 1 tomato, diced
- 1/2 red onion, chopped

- 1 teaspoon ground cumin
- 1/2 teaspoon chilli powder
- Salt and pepper to taste
- Vegan shredded cheese for topping

*Instructions:*
1. Turn the oven on and set it to 375°F (190°C).
2. Cooked rice, black beans, diced tomato, chopped red onion, ground cumin, chilli powder, salt, and pepper are all mixed in a bowl.
3. Fill each bell pepper with a mix of rice and black beans.
4. Put bell peppers stuffed in a baking dish and sprinkle vegan shredded cheese on top.
5. Bake for 20 to 25 minutes or until the peppers are soft and the cheese is melted.
6. Serve bell peppers with hot stuffing.

*Nutrition (per serving - 1 stuffed pepper):*
- Calories: 260
- Fat: 6g
- Carbohydrates: 44g
- Fiber: 12g
- Protein: 12g

## CREAMY CHIPOTLE SAUCE:

*Ingredients:*
- 1 cup raw cashews, soaked and drained
- 2 chipotle peppers in adobo sauce
- 2 tablespoons nutritional yeast
- Juice of 1 lime
- Salt and pepper to taste
- Water, as needed

*Instructions:*
1. Blend the soaked cashews, chipotle peppers in adobo sauce, nutritional yeast, lime juice, salt, and pepper until smooth.
2. Add water as needed to get the density you want.
3. Change the spices to your taste.
4. The creamy chipotle sauce can be used as a dip or a sauce.

*Nutrition (per serving - 2 tablespoons):*
- Calories: 60
- Fat: 4g
- Carbohydrates: 4g
- Fibre: 1g
- Protein: 2g

## ROASTED TOMATO SALSA:

*Ingredients:*
- 4 large tomatoes, roasted and peeled

- 1/2 red onion, chopped
- 1 jalapeno pepper, seeds removed and minced
- 2 cloves garlic, minced
- Juice of 1 lime
- 2 tablespoons chopped fresh cilantro
- Salt and pepper to taste

*Instructions:*
1. Put cooked tomatoes in a bowl and roughly mash them up.
2. Mix in chopped red onion, jalapeno pepper, garlic, chopped cilantro, and lime juice.
3. Add salt and pepper to taste.
4. Use the roasted tomato sauce as a topping or with tortilla chips.

*Nutrition (per serving - 1/4 cup):*
- Calories: 15
- Fat: 0g
- Carbohydrates: 4g
- Fibre: 1g
- Protein: 1g

## MANGO AND HABANERO SALSA:

*Ingredients:*
- 2 ripe mangoes, diced

- 1 habanero pepper, seeds removed and minced
- 1/4 red onion, finely chopped
- Juice of 1 lime
- 2 tablespoons chopped fresh cilantro
- Salt and pepper to taste

*Instructions:*
1. Diced mango, sliced habanero pepper, finely chopped red onion, lime juice, and chopped cilantro are mixed in a bowl.
2. Add salt and pepper to taste.
3. You can put the mango and jalapeño salsa on tacos or other grilled foods.

*Nutrition (per serving - 1/4 cup):*
- Calories: 30
- Fat: 0g
- Carbohydrates: 8g
- Fibre: 1g
- Protein: 0g

## VEGAN SOUR CREAM WITH LIME:

*Ingredients:*
- 1 cup raw cashews, soaked and drained
- Juice of 2 limes
- 1 tablespoon apple cider vinegar
- Salt to taste

- Water, as needed

*Instructions:*
1. Soaked cashews, lime juice, apple cider vinegar, and salt blend until smooth.
2. Add water as needed to get the density you want.
3. Lime juice and salt can be changed to taste.
4. You can put the vegan sour cream with lime on food or use it as a treat.

*Nutrition (per serving - 2 tablespoons):*
- Calories: 40
- Fat: 3g
- Carbohydrates: 2g
- Fibre: 0g
- Protein: 1g

## SALSA NEGRA (BLACK GARLIC SALSA):

*Ingredients:*
- 4 dried ancho chillies, stemmed and seeded
- 2 cloves black garlic
- 1 tablespoon soy sauce or tamari
- 1 tablespoon agave nectar
- Juice of 1 lime
- 1/4 cup water

*Instructions:*
1. Toast dried ancho chillies in a dry pan until they smell good.
2. Soak the toasted peppers for about 15 minutes in hot water. Drain.
3. Blend the peppers soaking in water, black garlic, soy sauce, agave nectar, lime juice, and water until smooth.
4. Taste and change the amount of soy sauce, agave nectar, and lime juice.
5. Serve the salsa negra as an exciting and tasty topping.

*Nutrition (per serving - 2 tablespoons):*
- Calories: 20
- Fat: 0g
- Carbohydrates: 5g
- Fibre: 1g
- Protein: 0g

## CILANTRO LIME CREMA:

*Ingredients:*
- 1 cup raw cashews, soaked and drained
- Juice of 2 limes
- 1 cup chopped fresh cilantro
- 1 clove garlic
- Salt and pepper to taste

- Water, as needed

**Instructions:**

1. Soaked cashews, lime juice, chopped cilantro, garlic, salt, and pepper blend until smooth.
2. Add water as needed to get the density you want.
3. Taste and adjust the lime juice, cilantro, and spices.
4. You can spread or dip it with the cilantro lime crema.

*Nutrition (per serving - 2 tablespoons):*
- Calories: 50
- Fat: 4g
- Carbohydrates: 3g
- Fibre: 0g
- Protein: 1g

## VEGAN RANCHERO SAUCE:

**Ingredients:**
- 1 tablespoon olive oil
- 1 onion, chopped
- 2 cloves garlic, minced
- 1 can (15 oz) diced tomatoes
- 1 teaspoon dried oregano

- 1/2 teaspoon ground cumin
- 1/4 teaspoon smoked paprika
- Salt and pepper to taste

**Instructions:**
1. Olive oil is heated in a pot over medium heat.
2. Add the chopped onion and cook it until it becomes clear.
3. Add the minced garlic and cook for another minute.
4. Mix diced tomatoes with their juice, dry oregano, ground cumin, smoked paprika, salt, and pepper.
5. Let the sauce simmer for 10–15 minutes to combine the flavours.
6. Blend the sauce until smooth with a hand blender.
7. Change the spices to your taste.
8. The veggie ranchero sauce goes well with enchiladas, tacos, and breakfast foods.

**Nutrition (per serving - 1/4 cup):**
- Calories: 20
- Fat: 1g
- Carbohydrates: 3g
- Fibre: 1g
- Protein: 1g

## POMEGRANATE AND JALAPENO SALSA:

**Ingredients:**

- 1 cup pomegranate seeds
- 1 jalapeno pepper, seeds removed and minced
- 1/4 red onion, finely chopped
- Juice of 1 lime
- 2 tablespoons chopped fresh cilantro
- Salt and pepper to taste

*Instructions:*

1. Mix chopped cilantro, lime juice, minced jalapeno pepper, finely cut red onion, and lime juice in a bowl.
2. Add salt and pepper to taste.
3. Toss them together well.
4. Serve the pomegranate and jalapeno salsa as an excellent topping.

*Nutrition (per serving - 1/4 cup):*

- Calories: 30
- Fat: 0g
- Carbohydrates: 7g
- Fibre: 1g
- Protein: 0g

## ROASTED TOMATILLO SALSA:

*Ingredients:*
- Six tomatillos, husked and rinsed
- 1/2 onion, chopped
- 1 jalapeno pepper, seeds removed
- 2 cloves garlic
- Juice of 1 lime
- 2 tablespoons chopped fresh cilantro
- Salt and pepper to taste

*Instructions:*
1. Get the grill ready.
2. Put the tomatillos, chopped onion, jalapeno pepper, and garlic on a baking sheet.
3. Broil the tomatillos until they are black and soft.
4. Roasted tomatillos, onion, jalapeño pepper, garlic, lime juice, and chopped cilantro are mixed in a blender until smooth.
5. Add salt and pepper to taste.
6. You can put the roasted tomatillo salsa on chips or use it as a sauce.

*Nutrition (per serving - 1/4 cup):*
- Calories: 15
- Fat: 0g
- Carbohydrates: 4g

- Fibre: 1g
- Protein: 0g

## ANCHO CHILI CASHEW CREAM:

*Ingredients:*
- 1 cup raw cashews, soaked and drained
- 2 dried ancho chillies, stemmed and seeded
- Juice of 1 lime
- 1 teaspoon ground cumin
- 1/2 teaspoon smoked paprika
- Salt and pepper to taste
- Water, as needed

*Instructions:*
1. Soaked cashews, dried ancho chillies, lime juice, ground cumin, smoked paprika, salt, and pepper are blended until smooth.
2. Add water as needed to get the density you want.
3. Taste and adjust the lime juice, spices, and herbs.
4. You can spray or dip it with the ancho chilli cashew cream.

*Nutrition (per serving - 2 tablespoons):*
- Calories: 60
- Fat: 4g
- Carbohydrates: 4g

- Fibre: 1g
- Protein: 2g

## VEGAN FLOUR TORTILLAS:

***Ingredients:***
- 2 cups all-purpose flour
- 1/2 teaspoon salt
- 1 teaspoon baking powder
- 1/4 cup vegetable oil
- 3/4 cup warm water

***Instructions:***
1. Mix all-purpose flour, salt, and baking powder in a bowl.
2. Add warm water and veggie oil. Mix until you get a dough.
3. Knead the dough for a few minutes on a floured surface.
4. Cut the dough into pieces about the size of a golf ball.
5. Each piece should be rolled into a thin, round tortilla.
6. Warm up a pan over medium heat. Cook each tortilla for about one to two minutes on each side until it is lightly browned and puffy.
7. The vegan flour tortillas should be served warm.

*Nutrition (per tortilla):*
- Calories: 120
- Fat: 5g
- Carbohydrates: 16g
- Fibre: 1g
- Protein: 2g

## BLUE CORN TORTILLAS:

*Ingredients:*
- 2 cups blue corn masa harina
- 1/2 teaspoon salt
- 1 1/4 cups warm water

*Instructions:*
1. Mix blue corn masa harina and salt in a bowl.
2. Gradually add the warm water and mix the dough until it is smooth.
3. Cut the dough into pieces about the size of a golf ball.
4. Use a tortilla press or rolling pin to flatten each piece into a round tortilla.
5. Warm up a pan over medium heat. Cook each tortilla for about one to two minutes on each side until it is done and has a slight brown colour.
6. The blue corn cakes should be served hot.

*Nutrition (per tortilla):*

- Calories: 50
- Fat: 0g
- Carbohydrates: 11g
- Fibre: 1g
- Protein: 1g

## SOPES WITH REFRIED BEANS AND GUACAMOLE:

*Ingredients:*
- 2 cups masa harina
- 1 teaspoon salt
- 1 1/4 cups warm water
- 1 cup refried beans
- 1 ripe avocado, mashed
- 1/4 red onion, finely chopped
- Juice of 1 lime
- Chopped fresh cilantro
- Vegan sour cream (optional)

*Instructions:*
1. Mix the masa harina and salt in a bowl.
2. Gradually add the warm water and mix the dough until it is smooth.
3. Cut the dough into pieces about the size of a golf ball.
4. Make a thick disk (sope) with slightly raised sides from each sample.

5. Each sope should be cooked in a pan over medium heat for about 2 to 3 minutes on each side until it is done and has a little bit of a brown colour.
6. Top each sope with refried beans, mashed avocado, freshly chopped red onion, lime juice, chopped cilantro, and vegan sour cream, if you want.

*Nutrition (per serving - 1 sope with toppings):*
- Calories: 120
- Fat: 5g
- Carbohydrates: 18g
- Fibre: 3g
- Protein: 3g

## VEGAN CONCHAS (SWEET BREAD):

*Ingredients:*
- 1 cup non-dairy milk
- 1/4 cup vegan butter, softened
- 1/4 cup agave nectar
- 2 teaspoons active dry yeast
- 3 cups all-purpose flour
- 1/2 teaspoon salt
- 1 teaspoon vanilla extract
- Vegan topping paste (coloured with cocoa powder, beet juice, etc.)

*Instructions:*
1. Warm the nondairy milk and mix in the agave nectar and vegan butter.
2. Sprinkle active dry yeast over the mixture and let it work for about 5 minutes.
3. Mix all-purpose flour and salt in a bowl.
4. Mix the yeast and vanilla extract and add it to the dry ingredients. Mix until you have a dough.
5. Knead the dough for a few minutes on a floured surface.
6. Put the dough in an oiled bowl, cover it, and let it rise for about an hour or two until it's doubled in size.
7. Each piece of dough should be shaped into a round concha.
8. Spread the vegan topping paste on each concha in the shape of a shell.
9. Bake the conchas for about 15 to 20 minutes at 350°F (175°C) in an oven that has already been hot.
10. Let the conchas cool down before you serve them.

*Nutrition (per concha):*
- Calories: 200
- Fat: 6g
- Carbohydrates: 32g

- Fibre: 1g
- Protein: 3g

## CORNBREAD WITH GREEN CHILIES:

***Ingredients:***
- 1 cup cornmeal
- 1 cup all-purpose flour
- 1 tablespoon baking powder
- 1/2 teaspoon salt
- 1 cup non-dairy milk
- 1/4 cup vegetable oil
- 1/4 cup agave nectar
- 1 can (4 oz) diced green chillies, drained

***Instructions:***
1. Turn the oven on and set it to 375°F (190°C). Grease a pan for baking.
2. Mix the cornmeal, flour, baking powder, and salt in a bowl.
3. Mix in nondairy milk, veggie oil, and agave nectar. Mix until everything is well blended.
4. Add diced green peppers and stir.
5. Pour the batter into the baking dish that has been coated.
6. Bake the cornbread for about 20 to 25 minutes, or until it's golden brown and a knife stuck in the middle comes out clean.

7. Let the cornbread cool down before cutting it into pieces and serving it.

***Nutrition (per serving - 1 slice):***
- Calories: 180
- Fat: 7g
- Carbohydrates: 26g
- Fiber: 2g
- Protein: 3g

## PUMPKIN SEED TORTILLAS:

***Ingredients:***
- 2 cups pumpkin seed flour
- 1/2 teaspoon salt
- 1 1/4 cups warm water

***Instructions:***
1. Mix the pumpkin seed flour and salt in a bowl.
2. Gradually add the warm water and mix the dough until it is smooth.
3. Cut the dough into pieces about the size of a golf ball.
4. Use a tortilla press or rolling pin to flatten each piece into a round tortilla.
5. Warm up a pan over medium heat. Cook each tortilla for about one to two minutes on each side until it is done and has a slight brown colour.

6. Warm up the rolls with pumpkin seeds.

*Nutrition (per tortilla):*
- Calories: 50
- Fat: 3g
- Carbohydrates: 2g
- Fibre: 1g
- Protein: 4g

## VEGAN BOLILLOS (CRUSTY ROLLS):

*Ingredients:*
- 1 1/2 cups warm water
- 2 teaspoons active dry yeast
- 1 teaspoon agave nectar
- 4 cups bread flour
- 1 teaspoon salt

*Instructions:*
1. Active dry yeast and agave juice need to be mixed with warm water. Give it about 5 minutes to work.
2. Mix bread flour and salt in a bowl.
3. Mix the yeast with the water and add it to the dry ingredients. Knead to make dough.
4. Knead the dough for a few minutes on a floured surface.

5. Put the dough in an oiled bowl, cover it, and let it rise for about an hour or two until it's doubled.
6. Punch the dough down and cut it into pieces.
7. Roll each piece into a bolillo and put it on a baking sheet.
8. Cover the rolls and let them rise for another half hour.
9. Turn the oven on and set it to 400°F (200°C).
10. Bake the bolillos for about 20 to 25 minutes or until golden brown and crusty.
11. Let the bolillos cool down before you serve them.

*Nutrition (per bolillo):*
- Calories: 200
- Fat: 1g
- Carbohydrates: 40g
- Fiber: 2g
- Protein: 6g

## CHIA AND FLAXSEED TORTILLAS:

*Ingredients:*
- 1 cup chia seeds
- 1 cup ground flaxseeds
- 1 teaspoon salt
- 1 1/2 cups warm water

*Instructions:*
1. Mix chia seeds, ground flaxseeds, and salt in a bowl.
2. Slowly add warm water and stir until everything is well mixed.
3. Let the mixture sit for about 15 to 20 minutes to thicken.
4. Put each piece of the mixture between two sheets of parchment paper.
5. Use a rolling pin to make each piece into a thin, round tortilla.
6. Warm up a pan over medium heat. Cook each tortilla for about one to two minutes on each side until it is done and has a slight brown colour.
7. The chia and flaxseed tortillas should be served warm.

*Nutrition (per tortilla):*
- Calories: 70
- Fat: 4g
- Carbohydrates: 7g
- Fibre: 6g
- Protein: 3g

## VEGAN TRES LECHES CAKE:

*Ingredients for Cake:*

- 2 cups all-purpose flour
- 1 cup granulated sugar
- 1 teaspoon baking powder
- 1/2 teaspoon baking soda
- 1/2 teaspoon salt
- 1 cup non-dairy milk
- 1/4 cup vegetable oil
- 1 tablespoon apple cider vinegar
- 1 teaspoon vanilla extract

**Ingredients for Tres Leches Mixture:**
- 1 can (14 oz) coconut milk
- 1 can (14 oz) sweetened condensed coconut milk
- 1/2 cup nondairy milk

**Ingredients for Whipped Coconut Cream Topping:**
- 1 can (14 oz) coconut cream, chilled
- 1/4 cup powdered sugar
- 1 teaspoon vanilla extract

**Instructions:**
1. Turn the oven on and set it to 350°F (175°C). Coat a baking pan with butter and flour.
2. Mix all-purpose flour, sugar, baking powder, baking soda, and salt in a bowl.
3. Mix in nondairy milk, veggie oil, apple cider vinegar, and vanilla extract. Mix until everything is well blended.

4. Pour the batter into the prepared baking pan and bake for about 25 to 30 minutes, or until a toothpick stuck in the middle comes out clean.
5. The tres leches blend is made by whisking together coconut milk, sweetened condensed coconut milk, and nondairy milk in a separate bowl.
6. Once the cake is done and has cooled a bit, use a fork to poke holes all over it.
7. Pour the recipe for tres leches over the cake and let it soak in.
8. The taste will blend better if you put the cake in the fridge for a few hours or overnight.
9. Spoon the solid coconut cream from the cold can into a bowl for the whipped coconut cream topping. Add vanilla flavour and powdered sugar. Whip until it's light and airy.
10. Spread the coconut cream on top of the cold cake.
11. Cut the vegan three-milk cake into pieces and serve it.

***Nutrition (per serving - 1 slice, without whipped cream):***
- Calories: 250
- Fat: 9g
- Carbohydrates: 38g
- Fibre: 1g
- Protein: 3g

## SWEET POTATO EMPANADAS:

*Ingredients for Dough:*
- 2 cups all-purpose flour
- 1/2 teaspoon salt
- 1/2 cup vegan butter, cold and cubed
- 1/2 cup cold water

*Ingredients for Filling:*
- 2 cups cooked and mashed sweet potatoes
- 1/4 cup brown sugar
- 1 teaspoon ground cinnamon
- 1/4 teaspoon ground nutmeg
- Pinch of salt

*Instructions:*
1. Mix all-purpose flour and salt in a bowl.
2. Mix in the vegan butter until it looks like coarse bits.
3. Mix while slowly adding cold water until the dough comes together.
4. Put the dough in a plastic bag and put it in the fridge for 30 minutes.
5. Mix mashed sweet potatoes, brown sugar, cinnamon powder, nutmeg powder, and a pinch of salt in a separate bowl for the filling.
6. Turn the oven on and set it to 375°F (190°C).

7. Roll out the cold dough on a floured surface and cut it into pieces.
8. On each dough round, put a spoonful of the sweet potato sauce.
9. Fold the dough over the filling and seal the sides by pressing them together. With a fork, you can crimp the edges.
10. Put the empanadas on a baking sheet and bake them for 20 to 25 minutes or until golden brown.
11. Let the empanadas with sweet potato cool down a bit before serving.

***Nutrition (per empanada):***
- Calories: 150
- Fat: 6g
- Carbohydrates: 22g
- Fiber: 2g
- Protein: 2g

## VEGAN CHURROS WITH CHOCOLATE SAUCE:

***Ingredients for Churros:***
- 1 cup water
- 1/2 cup vegan butter
- 1 tablespoon granulated sugar
- 1/4 teaspoon salt

- 1 cup all-purpose flour
- Vegetable oil for frying

**Ingredients for Cinnamon-Sugar Coating:**

- 1/2 cup granulated sugar
- 1 teaspoon ground cinnamon

**Ingredients for Chocolate Sauce:**

- 1/2 cup nondairy milk
- 1/2 cup vegan chocolate chips

*Instructions:*
1. Bring the water, vegan butter, sugar, and salt to a boil in a pot.
2. Take it off the heat and add plain flour. Mix until you get a dough.
3. Put the dough in a sewing bag with a star-shaped tip.
4. To fry, heat vegetable oil in a big pot.
5. Strips of dough are piped into the hot oil and fried until golden brown.
6. Take the churros out and put them on paper towels to dry.
7. For the coating, mix powdered sugar and cinnamon powder in a bowl. The cinnamon and sugar mixture is what you roll the fried churros in.

8. Heat nondairy milk in a pot for the chocolate sauce until it is hot but not boiling. Take it off the heat and add vegan chocolate chips. Mix until it's smooth.
9. The veggie churros should be served with warm chocolate sauce to dip them in.

*Nutrition (per serving - 2 churros with sauce):*
- Calories: 300
- Fat: 18g
- Carbohydrates: 32g
- Fibre: 1g
- Protein: 2g

## COCONUT TRES LECHES CAKE:

*Ingredients for Cake:*
- 2 cups all-purpose flour
- 1 1/2 cups granulated sugar
- 1 teaspoon baking powder
- 1/2 teaspoon baking soda
- 1/2 teaspoon salt
- 1 cup non-dairy milk
- 1/2 cup vegetable oil
- 2 teaspoons apple cider vinegar
- 1 teaspoon vanilla extract

**Ingredients for Tres Leches Mixture:**

- 1 can (14 oz) coconut milk
- 1 can (14 oz) sweetened condensed coconut milk
- 1/2 cup nondairy milk

**Ingredients for Coconut Whipped Cream Topping:**

- 1 can (14 oz) coconut cream, chilled
- 1/4 cup powdered sugar
- 1 teaspoon coconut extract

*Instructions:*
1. Turn the oven on and set it to 350°F (175°C). Coat a baking pan with butter and flour.
2. Mix all-purpose flour, sugar, baking powder, baking soda, and salt in a bowl.
3. Mix in nondairy milk, veggie oil, apple cider vinegar, and vanilla extract. Mix until everything is well blended.
4. Pour the batter into the prepared baking pan and bake for about 25 to 30 minutes, or until a toothpick stuck in the middle comes out clean.
5. The tres leches blend is made by whisking together coconut milk, sweetened condensed coconut milk, and nondairy milk in a separate bowl.

6. Once the cake is done and has cooled a bit, use a fork to poke holes all over it.
7. Pour the recipe for tres leches over the cake and let it soak in.
8. The taste will blend better if you put the cake in the fridge for a few hours or overnight.
9. Spoon the solid coconut cream from the cold can into a bowl for the coconut whipped cream topping. Powdered sugar and coconut flavour should be added. Whip until it's light and airy.
10. Spread the whipped coconut cream on top of the cold cake.
11. Cut the coconut tres leches cake into pieces and serve it.

*Nutrition (per serving - 1 slice, without whipped cream):*
- Calories: 250
- Fat: 9g
- Carbohydrates: 38g
- Fibre: 1g
- Protein: 3g

## CINNAMON-SUGAR BUÑUELOS:

*Ingredients:*
- 2 cups all-purpose flour
- 1 teaspoon baking powder
- 1/2 teaspoon salt

- 1/2 cup nondairy milk
- 1/4 cup vegetable oil
- 1/4 cup granulated sugar
- 1 teaspoon ground cinnamon

*Instructions:*
1. Mix all-purpose flour, baking powder, and salt in a bowl.
2. Add soy milk and oil made from plants. Mix until everything is well blended.
3. Knead the dough for a few minutes on a floured surface.
4. Cut the dough into pieces about the size of a golf ball.
5. Use a rolling pin to make each piece into a thin, round blue.
6. To fry, heat vegetable oil in a big pan.
7. Fry each below for about 1-2 minutes on each side or until golden brown and puffed up.
8. The buses need to be drained on paper towels.
9. Mix granulated sugar and cinnamon powder for the coating in a different bowl. Cinnamon and sugar are mixed in a bowl.
10. Warm up the bunuelos with cinnamon and sugar.

**Nutrition (per buñuelo):**

- Calories: 120
- Fat: 4g
- Carbohydrates: 19g
- Fiber: 1g
- Protein: 2g

## VEGAN ARROZ CON LECHE:

*Ingredients:*
- 1 cup Arborio rice
- 4 cups nondairy milk
- 1/2 cup granulated sugar
- 1 teaspoon vanilla extract
- 1/2 teaspoon ground cinnamon
- Pinch of salt
- Raisins and ground cinnamon for garnish

*Instructions:*
1. Mix Arborio rice, nondairy milk, granulated sugar, vanilla extract, cinnamon powder, and a pinch of salt in a pot.
2. Over medium heat, bring the mixture to a slow boil.
3. Turn the heat down to low and cook, stirring often, for about 25 to 30 minutes or until the rice is soft and the sauce has thickened.
4. Take the rice and milk off the heat and let it cool down.

5. You can serve the arroz con leche hot or cold, with a sprinkle of ground cinnamon and some raisins on top.

**Nutrition (per serving):**
- Calories: 200
- Fat: 2g
- Carbohydrates: 40g
- Fibre: 1g
- Protein: 4g

## CHOCOLATE AVOCADO MOUSSE:

**Ingredients:**
- 2 ripe avocados, peeled and pitted
- 1/2 cup cocoa powder
- 1/4 cup agave nectar
- 1 teaspoon vanilla extract
- Pinch of salt
- Nondairy milk, as needed

**Instructions:**
1. Blend ripe avocados, chocolate powder, agave nectar, vanilla extract, and a pinch of salt in a food processor until the mixture is smooth.
2. Add nondairy milk as needed to get the mousse-like texture you want.
3. Taste how sweet something is and how cocoa tastes.

4. Before serving, put the chocolate avocado mousse in the fridge for at least an hour.
5. Serve the mousse in cups or bowls for each person.

*Nutrition (per serving - 1/2 cup):*
- Calories: 180
- Fat: 12g
- Carbohydrates: 19g
- Fibre: 7g
- Protein: 3g

## MANGO SORBET WITH CHILI-LIME SALT:

*Ingredients for Sorbet:*
- 3 ripe mangoes, peeled and diced
- 1/4 cup agave nectar
- Juice of 1 lime

**Ingredients for Chili-Lime Salt:**

- 1 teaspoon chilli powder
- Zest of 1 lime
- Pinch of salt

*Instructions:*
1. Blend ripe mangoes, agave nectar, and lime juice until smooth.

2. Put the mango mixture in a jar and freeze it, stirring it occasionally until solid.
3. Mix chilli-lime salt, chilli powder, lime zest, and a pinch of salt in a bowl.
4. Sprinkle chilli-lime salt on top of scoops of mango sorbet.

*Nutrition (per serving - 1/2 cup sorbet with chilli-lime salt):*
- Calories: 100
- Fat: 0g
- Carbohydrates: 25g
- Fiber: 2g
- Protein: 1g

## AGUA FRESCA POPSICLES (HORCHATA, JAMAICA, TAMARIND):

*Ingredients for Horchata Popsicles:*
- 2 cups horchata
- 2 tablespoons agave nectar

### Ingredients for Jamaica Popsicles:

- 2 cups hibiscus tea (Jamaica), sweetened to taste

### Ingredients for Tamarind Popsicles:

- 2 cups tamarind juice, sweetened to taste

***Instructions:***
1. To make them, follow the recipes for horchata, Jamaican hibiscus tea, and tamarind juice.
2. You can make the horchata, hibiscus tea, and tamarind juice as sweet as you like.
3. Pour the liquids of each taste into the popsicle moulds.
4. Put the popsicles in the freezer until they are solid, which usually takes 4-6 hours or overnight.

***Nutrition (per popsicle):***
- Calories: 40-60 (depending on flavour)
- Fat: 0g
- Carbohydrates: 10-15g (depending on taste)
- Fibre: 0-1g (depending on preference)
- Protein: 0-1g (depending on preference)

## VEGAN FLAN WITH CARAMEL SAUCE:

***Ingredients for Flan:***
- 1 cup raw cashews, soaked and drained
- 1 can (14 oz) coconut milk
- 1/2 cup granulated sugar
- 1 teaspoon vanilla extract
- Pinch of salt

## Ingredients for Caramel Sauce:

- 1/2 cup granulated sugar

*Instructions:*
1. Turn the oven on and set it to 350°F (175°C).
2. Blend the soaked cashews, coconut milk, sugar, vanilla extract, and a pinch of salt until the mixture is smooth.
3. Melt granulated sugar in a pot over medium heat to make the caramel sauce. Stir the sugar until it turns a golden colour.
4. Pour the caramel sauce into flan pans for each person.
5. Pour the blend of cashews and coconut over the caramel sauce in the moulds.
6. Put the moulds in a larger baking dish that has water in it (this is called a "water bath").
7. Bake the flan for 30–35 minutes or until it's set.
8. Let the flan cool, then put it in the fridge for a few hours or overnight.
9. Carefully turn each flan pan upside down onto a plate to remove the flan and caramel.

*Nutrition (per serving - 1 flan):*
- Calories: 200
- Fat: 11g
- Carbohydrates: 25g
- Fibre: 1g

- Protein: 3g

## MEXICAN HOT CHOCOLATE BROWNIES:

*Ingredients:*
- 1 cup all-purpose flour
- 1/2 cup cocoa powder
- 1 teaspoon ground cinnamon
- 1/4 teaspoon cayenne pepper (optional)
- 1/2 teaspoon baking powder
- 1/2 teaspoon salt
- 1/2 cup vegan butter, melted
- 1 cup granulated sugar
- 1/4 cup nondairy milk
- 1 teaspoon vanilla extract

*Instructions:*
1. Turn the oven on and set it to 350°F (175°C). Coat a baking pan with butter and flour.
2. Mix all-purpose flour, cocoa powder, cinnamon powder, chilli pepper (if using), baking powder, and salt in a bowl.
3. Mix together vegan butter that has been melted, granulated sugar, nondairy milk, and vanilla extract in another bowl.
4. Mix the wet and dry ingredients until they are just mixed.

5. Pour the cookie batter into the pan set up for baking and spread it out evenly.
6. Bake for about 25 to 30 minutes, or until a toothpick put into the middle comes out with a few moist crumbs.
7. Let the brownies cool down before you cut them and serve them.

*Nutrition (per brownie):*
- Calories: 150
- Fat: 7g
- Carbohydrates: 21g
- Fiber: 2g
- Protein: 2g

## VEGAN PINEAPPLE EMPANADAS:

*Ingredients for Dough:*
- 2 cups all-purpose flour
- 1/2 teaspoon salt
- 1/2 cup vegan butter, cold and cubed
- 1/2 cup cold water

**Ingredients for Filling:**

- 2 cups diced pineapple
- 1/4 cup granulated sugar
- 1 tablespoon cornstarch

- Juice of 1 lime

***Instructions:***
1. Mix all-purpose flour and salt in a bowl.
2. Mix in the vegan butter until it looks like coarse bits.
3. Mix while slowly adding cold water until the dough comes together.
4. Put the dough in a plastic bag and put it in the fridge for 30 minutes.
5. Put diced pineapple, sugar, cornstarch, and lime juice in a pot for the filling.
6. Over medium heat, cook the filling until it thickens and the pineapple is soft.
7. Turn the oven on and set it to 375°F (190°C).
8. Roll out the cold dough on a floured surface and cut it into pieces.
9. On each bread round, put a spoonful of pineapple filling.
10. Fold the dough over the filling and seal the sides by pressing them together. With a fork, you can crimp the edges.
11. Put the empanadas on a baking sheet and bake them for 20 to 25 minutes or until golden brown.
12. Let the pineapple empanadas cool down a bit before you serve them.

*Nutrition (per empanada):*
- Calories: 150
- Fat: 6g
- Carbohydrates: 22g
- Fiber: 1g
- Protein: 1g

## CLASSIC HORCHATA:

*Ingredients:*
- 1 cup long-grain white rice
- 3 cups water
- 1 cinnamon stick
- 1/4 cup granulated sugar
- 1 teaspoon vanilla extract
- 1 cup nondairy milk (almond, rice, or coconut)

*Instructions:*
1. Rinse the rice well, then put it and the cinnamon stick in a water bowl for at least 6 hours or overnight.
2. Mix the rice that has been soaked, cinnamon stick, and water until it is smooth. Use a fine mesh sieve or cheesecloth to strain.
3. Stir in the granulated sugar, vanilla extract, and nondairy milk.

4. Serve over ice, and add some ground cinnamon on top if you want.

*Nutrition (per serving - 1 cup):*
- Calories: 120
- Fat: 2g
- Carbohydrates: 23g
- Fibre: 1g
- Protein: 2g

## Watermelon Agua Fresca: Ingredients:

- 4 cups cubed watermelon
- 2 cups water
- 2 tablespoons agave nectar
- Juice of 1 lime

*Instructions:*
1. Blend watermelon and water until smooth.
2. Strain through a fine mesh sieve or cheesecloth.
3. Stir in agave nectar and lime juice.
4. Serve over ice with a slice of lime.

*Nutrition (per serving - 1 cup):*
- Calories: 50
- Fat: 0g
- Carbohydrates: 13g
- Fibre: 1g
- Protein: 1g

## VEGAN MEXICAN COFFEE:

*Ingredients:*
- 1 cup strong brewed coffee
- 1/4 cup nondairy milk (almond, soy, or oat)
- 1 tablespoon agave nectar
- 1/4 teaspoon ground cinnamon
- Vegan whipped cream (optional)

*Instructions:*
1. Coffee should be strong.
2. Warm the nondairy milk and mix in the agave juice and cinnamon powder.
3. Pour the brewed coffee into a cup and top it with the nondairy milk blend that has been heated.
4. You can add cinnamon and vegan whipped cream to the top if you want to.

*Nutrition (per serving - 1 cup):*
- Calories: 20
- Fat: 1g
- Carbohydrates: 3g
- Protein: 0g

## HIBISCUS TEA (AGUA DE JAMAICA):

*Ingredients:*

- 1 cup dried hibiscus flowers
- 4 cups water
- 1/4 cup agave nectar
- Juice of 1 lime

*Instructions:*
1. Pour boiling water over dried hibiscus flowers.
2. Let the mixture sit for 20 to 30 minutes, then strain.
3. Mix in lime juice and agave nectar.
4. Place on ice.

*Nutrition (per serving - 1 cup):*
- Calories: 20
- Fat: 0g
- Carbohydrates: 5g
- Protein: 0g

## SPICY MANGO MARGARITA:

*Ingredients:*
- 2 oz silver tequila
- 1 oz fresh lime juice
- 1 oz mango puree
- 1/2 oz agave nectar
- Sliced jalapeno (optional, for spice)

*Instructions:*
1. Combine tequila, lime juice, mango puree, and agave nectar in a shaker.

2. Shake well and strain into a glass filled with ice.
3. Garnish with sliced jalapeno for a spicy kick.

*Nutrition (per serving):*
- Calories: 150
- Carbohydrates: 15g
- Protein: 0g

## CUCUMBER LIME AGUA FRESCA:

**Ingredients:**
- 2 cups cucumber, peeled and chopped
- 4 cups water
- 2 tablespoons agave nectar
- Juice of 2 limes

**Instructions:**
1. Blend cucumber and water until smooth.
2. Strain through a fine mesh sieve or cheesecloth.
3. Stir in agave nectar and lime juice.
4. Serve over ice.

*Nutrition (per serving - 1 cup):*
- Calories: 20
- Fat: 0g
- Carbohydrates: 5g
- Protein: 0g

## VEGAN PIÑA COLADA:

*Ingredients:*
- 2 oz white rum (optional)
- 1 cup pineapple chunks
- 1/2 cup coconut milk
- 1/2 cup coconut water
- 1 tablespoon agave nectar

*Instructions:*
1. Blend all ingredients until smooth.
2. Serve over ice, optionally garnished with a pineapple slice.

*Nutrition (per serving):*
- Calories: 150
- Fat: 4g
- Carbohydrates: 25g
- Fiber: 2g
- Protein: 1g

## MINTY MOJITO MOCKTAIL:

*Ingredients:*
- 1/2 lime, cut into wedges
- 8-10 fresh mint leaves
- 1 tablespoon agave nectar
- Club soda

*Instructions:*

1. Muddle lime wedges, mint leaves, and agave nectar in a glass.
2. Fill the glass with ice and top with club soda.
3. Stir gently and garnish with a sprig of mint.

**Nutrition (per serving):**
- Calories: 20
- Carbohydrates: 5g
- Protein: 0g

## MEXICAN HOT CHOCOLATE:

**Ingredients:**
- 2 cups nondairy milk (almond, soy, or oat)
- 2 tablespoons cocoa powder
- 2 tablespoons granulated sugar
- 1/2 teaspoon ground cinnamon
- Pinch of cayenne pepper (optional)
- Vegan whipped cream (optional)

**Instructions:**
1. In a pot, heat nondairy milk over medium heat.
2. Mix in the cocoa powder, sugar, cinnamon, and chilli pepper, if you're using it.
3. Keep whisking until everything is well mixed and hot.
4. Pour into mugs and top with cocoa powder and vegan whipped cream.

**Nutrition (per serving - 1 cup):**

- Calories: 100
- Fat: 2g
- Carbohydrates: 18g
- Fibre: 3g
- Protein: 2g

## PRICKLY PEAR CACTUS SMOOTHIE:

*Ingredients:*
- 1 prickly pear cactus fruit, peeled and diced
- 1 cup frozen mixed berries
- 1 banana
- 1 cup nondairy milk (almond, soy, or coconut)
- 1 tablespoon agave nectar

*Instructions:*
1. Blend all ingredients until smooth.
2. Serve in a glass, optionally garnished with diced prickly pear cactus fruit.

*Nutrition (per serving):*
- Calories: 150
- Fat: 1g
- Carbohydrates: 35g
- Fibre: 5g
- Protein: 2g

## VEGAN CHILAQUILES:

*Ingredients:*
- 6 corn tortillas, cut into triangles
- 1 cup red or green salsa
- 1 cup cooked black beans
- 1 cup diced tofu scramble (see Tofu Scramble Breakfast Tacos recipe)
- 1/4 cup chopped cilantro
- Vegan sour cream (optional)
- Sliced jalapenos (optional)

*Instructions:*
1. Turn the oven on and set it to 375°F (190°C).
1. Spread the pieces of corn tortilla on a baking sheet and bake for about 10 to 12 minutes or until they are crispy.
2. Heat the salsa over medium heat in a big pan. Add the pieces of baked tortilla and stir to coat.
3. Stir gently to mix in the cooked black beans and tofu scramble.
4. Cook everything for a few minutes until it's all hot.
5. Serve hot with chopped cilantro, sliced chillies, and vegan sour cream.

*Nutrition (per serving):*
- Calories: 250

- Fat: 6g
- Carbohydrates: 40g
- Fibre: 10g
- Protein: 12g

## TOFU SCRAMBLE BREAKFAST TACOS:

*Ingredients:*
- 8 small corn tortillas
- 1 block (14 oz) firm tofu, crumbled
- 1/2 bell pepper, diced
- 1/2 onion, diced
- 2 cloves garlic, minced
- 1 teaspoon ground cumin
- 1/2 teaspoon turmeric
- Salt and pepper, to taste
- Chopped fresh cilantro
- Sliced avocado

*Instructions:*
1. Bell pepper, onion, and garlic are cooked in a pan over medium heat until soft.
2. Add chopped tofu, ground cumin, turmeric, salt, and pepper to the pan. Cook, stirring occasionally, for about 5–7 minutes, until warm and a little bit brown.

3. The corn tortillas can be heated in a dry pan or the microwave.
4. Scrambled tofu, chopped cilantro, and sliced avocado can make tacos.

*Nutrition (per serving - 2 tacos):*
- Calories: 250
- Fat: 10g
- Carbohydrates: 28g
- Fibre: 7g
- Protein: 15g

## SWEET POTATO AND BLACK BEAN BREAKFAST BURRITOS:

*Ingredients:*
- 4 large whole wheat tortillas
- 2 cups cooked and mashed sweet potatoes
- 1 cup cooked black beans
- 1/2 teaspoon ground cumin
- Salt and pepper, to taste
- Sliced avocado
- Salsa

*Instructions:*
1. The tortillas can be warmed in a dry pan or the microwave.

2. Mix mashed sweet potatoes, cooked black beans, cumin powder, salt, and pepper in a bowl.
3. Spread the blend of sweet potato and black beans on each tortilla.
4. Slice an avocado and mix in salsa.
5. Make burritos by folding the tortillas' sides and rolling them up.

*Nutrition (per burrito):*
- Calories: 300
- Fat: 5g
- Carbohydrates: 55g
- Fiber: 12g
- Protein: 10g

## VEGAN BREAKFAST ENCHILADAS:

*Ingredients:*
- 8 small corn tortillas
- 2 cups cooked and mashed sweet potatoes
- 1 cup black beans, cooked and drained
- 1 cup vegan cheese, shredded
- 1 cup red or green salsa
- Chopped fresh cilantro
- Sliced avocado

*Instructions:*
1. Turn the oven on and set it to 375°F (190°C).

2. The corn tortillas can be heated in a dry pan or the microwave.
3. Mix mashed sweet potatoes and black beans in a bowl.
4. Spread a spoonful of salsa on each tortilla, then add the sweet potato and black bean combination.
5. The tortillas should be rolled up and put in a baking dish.
6. Pour more salsa over the enchiladas and sprinkle them with vegan cheese.
7. Bake for 15 to 20 minutes or until the cheese is melted and bubbly.
8. Before serving, top with chopped cilantro and slices of avocado.

*Nutrition (per serving - 2 enchiladas):*
- Calories: 350
- Fat: 10g
- Carbohydrates: 55g
- Fiber: 12g
- Protein: 15g

## MEXICAN-INSPIRED AVOCADO TOAST:

*Ingredients:*
- 2 slices whole grain bread, toasted

- 1 ripe avocado, mashed
- 1/4 teaspoon ground cumin
- Salt and pepper, to taste
- Sliced radishes
- Chopped fresh cilantro
- Red pepper flakes (optional)

*Instructions:*
1. Mix the ground cumin, salt, and pepper into the mashed avocado in a bowl.
2. Spread the avocado spread on the slices of bread that have been toasted.
3. Radish slices and chopped cilantro go on top.
4. Add some heat with red pepper flakes.

*Nutrition (per serving - 1 slice):*
- Calories: 150
- Fat: 10g
- Carbohydrates: 15g
- Fibre: 5g
- Protein: 3g

## VEGAN BREAKFAST QUESADILLAS:

*Ingredients:*
- 4 small whole wheat tortillas
- 1 cup cooked and diced potatoes
- 1/2 cup black beans, cooked and drained
- 1/2 cup chopped bell peppers

- 1/4 cup diced red onion
- 1/2 teaspoon ground cumin
- Salt and pepper, to taste
- Vegan cheese, shredded
- Salsa

**Instructions:**
1. Diced potatoes, black beans, bell peppers, and red onion are cooked together in a pan until the potatoes are golden and crispy.
2. Add salt, pepper, and ground cumin.
3. The tortillas can be warmed in a dry pan or the microwave.
4. Split the blend of potatoes and black beans between two tortillas.
5. On top of the mixture, sprinkle vegan cheese and cover with the rest of the tortillas.
6. Over medium heat, cook the quesadillas until the cheese is melted and the tortillas are crisp.
7. Serve the slices with salsa.

**Nutrition (per quesadilla):**
- Calories: 300
- Fat: 8g
- Carbohydrates: 48g
- Fiber: 10g
- Protein: 12g

## CHORIZO-SPICED TOFU BREAKFAST BOWL:

Ingredients:

- 1 block (14 oz) firm tofu, crumbled
- 1 teaspoon olive oil
- 1/2 teaspoon ground cumin
- 1/2 teaspoon smoked paprika
- 1/4 teaspoon garlic powder
- 1/4 teaspoon onion powder
- Salt and pepper, to taste
- Sliced avocado
- Salsa
- Chopped fresh cilantro

**Instructions:**
1. Heat the olive oil in a pan and cook the crumbled tofu until it gets a little bit crispy.
2. Add the ground cumin, smoked paprika, garlic powder, onion powder, salt, and pepper. Wait one more minute.
3. Serve the chorizo-flavoured tofu in a bowl with chopped cilantro, sliced avocado, and salsa.

**Nutrition (per serving):**
- Calories: 200
- Fat: 12g
- Carbohydrates: 8g

- Fibre: 3g
- Protein: 15g

## VEGAN HUEVOS RANCHEROS:

*Ingredients:*
- 2 small corn tortillas
- 1/2 cup cooked black beans
- 1/4 cup red or green salsa
- 1/4 cup diced tomatoes
- 1/4 cup diced red onion
- Sliced avocado
- Chopped fresh cilantro

*Instructions:*
1. Warm the corn tortillas in a dry skillet or microwave.
2. Spread black beans on the tortillas and top with salsa, tomatoes, and red onion.
3. Garnish with sliced avocado and chopped cilantro.

*Nutrition (per serving - 2 tortillas):*
- Calories: 250
- Fat: 5g
- Carbohydrates: 40g
- Fibre: 10g
- Protein: 10g

## CINNAMON-SUGAR CHURRO PANCAKES:

*Ingredients:*

- 1 cup all-purpose flour
- 2 tablespoons granulated sugar
- 1 teaspoon baking powder
- 1/2 teaspoon ground cinnamon
- 1 cup nondairy milk (almond, soy, or oat)
- 1 tablespoon apple cider vinegar
- 1 teaspoon vanilla extract
- Vegan butter or oil for cooking
- Cinnamon-sugar mixture (2 tablespoons granulated sugar + 1 teaspoon ground cinnamon)

*Instructions:*

1. Mix the flour, sugar, baking powder, and cinnamon in a bowl.
2. Mix non-dairy milk, apple cider vinegar, and vanilla extract separately. Let it sit for a little while.
3. Mix the wet and dry ingredients until they are just mixed.
4. Put vegan butter or oil in a pan and heat it over medium heat.
5. Pour pancake batter into the pan and cook until bubbles are on the top.

6. Turn the pancakes over and cook until they are golden brown.
7. Before serving, you can dip the pancakes in the cinnamon-sugar mixture.

*Nutrition (per serving - 2 pancakes):*
- Calories: 250
- Fat: 5g
- Carbohydrates: 45g
- Fiber: 2g
- Protein: 5g

## MEXICAN-INSPIRED TOFU BENEDICT:

*Ingredients:*
- 2 English muffins, toasted and halved
- 1 block (14 oz) firm tofu, sliced into thick rectangles
- 1 tablespoon olive oil
- 1/2 teaspoon ground cumin
- 1/2 teaspoon smoked paprika
- Salt and pepper, to taste
- Vegan hollandaise sauce (see below)
- Chopped fresh cilantro
- Sliced avocado

**Vegan Hollandaise Sauce:**

- 1/2 cup raw cashews, soaked and drained
- 1/2 cup water
- Juice of 1 lemon
- 1/2 teaspoon Dijon mustard
- 1/4 teaspoon ground turmeric
- Salt and pepper, to taste

**Instructions:**
1. Warm olive oil in a pan and cook tofu slices until golden. Add salt, pepper, ground cumin, and smoked paprika.
2. Make the vegan hollandaise sauce: Blend the water, lemon juice, Dijon mustard, ground turmeric, salt, and pepper with the soaked nuts until smooth.
3. To put it all together, put halves of toasted English muffins on plates. Sautéed slices of tofu can go on top.
4. Pour hollandaise sauce made from plants over the tofu.
5. Add chopped cilantro and thin slices of avocado.

**Nutrition (per serving - 1 Benedict):**
- Calories: 400
- Fat: 25g
- Carbohydrates: 30g
- Fibre: 7g

- Protein: 20g

## VEGAN ELOTE (GRILLED CORN):

***Ingredients:***
- 4 ears of corn, husks removed
- 1/4 cup vegan mayonnaise
- 2 tablespoons nutritional yeast
- 1 teaspoon ground cumin
- Juice of 1 lime
- Chilli powder for sprinkling
- Chopped fresh cilantro

***Instructions:***
1. Grill or roast the corn until slightly charred.
2. Mix vegan mayonnaise, nutritional yeast, ground cumin, and lime juice in a bowl.
3. Spread the mayo mixture over the grilled corn.
4. Sprinkle with chilli powder and chopped cilantro before serving.

***Nutrition (per serving - 1 ear of corn):***
- Calories: 150
- Fat: 6g
- Carbohydrates: 25g
- Fibre: 4g
- Protein: 4g

# TOFU AND VEGETABLE TLAYUDAS:

*Ingredients:*

- 2 large whole wheat tortillas (tlayudas)
- 1 block (14 oz) firm tofu, sliced into thin rectangles
- 1 teaspoon olive oil
- 1/2 teaspoon ground cumin
- 1/2 teaspoon smoked paprika
- Salt and pepper, to taste
- 1/2 cup refried beans (see Vegan Refried Beans recipe)
- 1/4 cup diced red onion
- Sliced avocado
- Salsa
- Chopped fresh cilantro

*Instructions:*

1. Warm olive oil in a pan and cook tofu slices until golden. Add salt, pepper, ground cumin, and smoked paprika.
2. The tortillas can be warmed in a dry pan or the microwave.
3. On one side of each tortilla, spread refried beans.
4. Top with pieces of sautéed tofu, diced red onion, sliced avocado, salsa, and chopped cilantro.

5. The tortillas are served folded in half.

***Nutrition (per tlayuda):***
- Calories: 400
- Fat: 15g
- Carbohydrates: 45g
- Fiber: 10g
- Protein: 20g

## VEGAN SOPES WITH PICO DE GALLO:

***Ingredients:***
- 8 small corn slopes (or use small corn tortillas)
- 1 cup refried beans (see Vegan Refried Beans recipe)
- 1 cup diced tofu scramble (see Tofu Scramble Breakfast Tacos recipe)
- 1 cup pico de gallo (diced tomatoes, red onion, cilantro, lime juice)
- Sliced avocado
- Chopped fresh cilantro

***Instructions:***
1. Warm the corn slopes in a dry skillet or microwave.
2. Spread refried beans on each sope.
3. Top with diced tofu scramble, pico de gallo, sliced avocado, and chopped cilantro.

*Nutrition (per Sope):*
- Calories: 200
- Fat: 8g
- Carbohydrates: 25g
- Fibre: 5g
- Protein: 10g

## SPICY MANGO WITH CHILI POWDER:

**Ingredients:**
- 2 ripe mangoes, peeled and sliced
- Chilli powder, to taste
- Lime wedges

**Instructions:**
1. Arrange sliced mangoes on a plate.
1. Sprinkle chilli powder over the mango slices.
2. Serve with lime wedges for squeezing.

*Nutrition (per serving - 1 mango):*
- Calories: 100
- Fat: 0g
- Carbohydrates: 25g
- Fibre: 3g
- Protein: 1g

## VEGAN TACOS DE CANASTA:

**Ingredients:**

- 8 small corn tortillas
- 2 cups cooked and seasoned potato cubes
- 1 cup cooked and seasoned black beans
- Sliced avocado
- Sliced radishes
- Chopped fresh cilantro

*Instructions:*
1. Warm the corn tortillas in a dry skillet or microwave.
2. Fill each tortilla with seasoned potato cubes and black beans.
3. Top with sliced avocado, sliced radishes, and chopped cilantro.

*Nutrition (per taco):*
- Calories: 200
- Fat: 5g
- Carbohydrates: 35g
- Fibre: 8g
- Protein: 6g

## Roasted Chile and Lime Popcorn: Ingredients:

- 1/2 cup popcorn kernels
- 2 tablespoons olive oil
- 1 teaspoon chilli powder
- Zest of 1 lime
- Salt, to taste

*Instructions:*
1. Turn the oven on and set it to 350°F (175°C).
2. Olive oil the popcorn nuts and spread them out on a baking sheet.
3. Bake the popcorn for about 10 to 12 minutes until it has popped and turned a light brown.
4. Mix chilli powder, lime juice, and salt in a bowl.
5. Toss the spice mix with the roasted popcorn.

*Nutrition (per serving - 1 cup):*
- Calories: 50
- Fat: 2g
- Carbohydrates: 7g
- Fibre: 1g
- Protein: 1g

## VEGAN GORDITAS:

*Ingredients:*
- 8 small corn gorditas (thick tortillas)
- 1 cup cooked and seasoned black beans
- 1 cup diced tomatoes
- 1/2 cup shredded lettuce
- Sliced avocado
- Salsa
- Chopped fresh cilantro

*Instructions:*

1. Warm the corn gorditas in a dry skillet or microwave.
2. Fill each gordita with seasoned black beans, diced tomatoes, shredded lettuce, sliced avocado, salsa, and chopped cilantro.

*Nutrition (per gordita):*
- Calories: 200
- Fat: 5g
- Carbohydrates: 35g
- Fiber: 8g
- Protein: 8g

## STREET-STYLE ROASTED NUTS WITH SPICES:

*Ingredients:*
- 1 cup mixed nuts (almonds, peanuts, cashews)
- 1 tablespoon olive oil
- 1 teaspoon chilli powder
- 1/2 teaspoon ground cumin
- 1/4 teaspoon cayenne pepper (adjust to taste)
- Salt, to taste

*Instructions:*
1. Turn the oven on and set it to 350°F (175°C).

2. Spread mixed nuts on a baking sheet and toss them with olive oil.
3. About 10 to 15 minutes, stirring every so often.
4. Mix the chilli powder, ground cumin, cayenne pepper, and salt in a bowl.
5. Mix the spice mix with the roasted nuts.

*Nutrition (per serving - 1/4 cup):*
- Calories: 150
- Fat: 13g
- Carbohydrates: 5g
- Fiber: 2g
- Protein: 5g

## VEGAN QUESADILLA WITH SALSA ROJA:

*Ingredients:*
- 2 small whole wheat tortillas
- 1 cup vegan cheese, shredded
- 1/4 cup red or green salsa

*Instructions:*
1. Put one tortilla on a pan that is heated to medium.
2. Cover the bread with half of the vegan cheese.
3. Spread salsa on the cheese, then put the rest of the cheese on top.

4. Put the second tortilla on top and cook until the bottom is crispy.
5. Turn the quesadilla over and cook until the cheese is melted and the other side is crispy.
6. Cut it up and serve.

*Nutrition (per quesadilla):*
- Calories: 350
- Fat: 15g
- Carbohydrates: 35g
- Fiber: 7g
- Protein: 15g

## CHURRO BITES WITH CARAMEL DIPPING SAUCE:

*Ingredients:*
- 1 cup all-purpose flour
- 2 tablespoons granulated sugar
- 1 teaspoon ground cinnamon
- 1/4 teaspoon salt
- 1 cup water
- 1/4 cup vegan butter
- 1 teaspoon vanilla extract
- Oil for frying

**Caramel Dipping Sauce:**

- 1/2 cup coconut cream
- 1/2 cup brown sugar
- 1 teaspoon vanilla extract

*Instructions:*
1. Whisk together the flour, sugar, cinnamon powder, and salt in a bowl.
2. Bring water and vegan butter to a boil in a pot. Take the pool off the heat and mix in the vanilla extract.
3. Mix the wet and dry ingredients until they are smooth.
4. To fry, heat oil in a big pan.
5. Drop spoonfuls of the churro batter into the hot oil and cook until golden brown.
6. On paper towels, drain the churro bites.
7. Make the caramel sauce for dipping: Heat the coconut cream and brown sugar together until the sugar is melted. Add the vanilla extract and mix.
8. Dip churro bites in caramel sauce and serve.

*Nutrition (per serving - 4 churro bites with sauce):*
- Calories: 300
- Fat: 15g
- Carbohydrates: 40g
- Fibre: 1g
- Protein: 2g

## VEGAN DAY OF THE DEAD SUGAR SKULL COOKIES:

*Ingredients:*

- 2 cups all-purpose flour
- 1/2 cup vegan butter, softened
- 1/2 cup granulated sugar
- 1 flax egg (1 tablespoon ground flaxseed + 3 tablespoons water)
- 1 teaspoon vanilla extract
- 1/4 teaspoon almond extract
- 1/4 teaspoon salt
- Vegan royal icing (see below)

**Vegan Royal Icing:**

- 1 cup powdered sugar
- 1-2 tablespoons nondairy milk
- Food colouring (optional)

*Instructions:*

1. Cream vegan butter and granulated sugar together in a bowl.
2. Add the flax egg, vanilla, almond, and salt extracts. Blend well.
3. Mix in the flour bit by bit until a dough forms.

4. Roll out the dough on a floured surface and use cookie cutters to make sugar skull shapes.
5. Put the sugar skull cookies on a baking sheet and bake them at 350°F (175°C) for 10–12 minutes, until the sides are golden.
6. Prepare the vegan royal icing: Mix powdered sugar and nondairy milk until smooth. If you want, you can add food colours.
7. Put royal icing on the sugar skull cookies after they have cooled.

*Nutrition (per cookie):*
- Calories: 150
- Fat: 6g
- Carbohydrates: 23g
- Fibre: 1g
- Protein: 2g

## VEGAN POSADAS FRUIT PUNCH:

*Ingredients:*
- 4 cups fruit juice (orange, pineapple, or a combination)
- 1 cup cranberry juice
- 1/4 cup lime juice
- 1/4 cup agave nectar
- 2 cups sparkling water or Club soda

*Instructions:*

1. Mix fruit juice, cranberry juice, lime juice, and agave nectar in a pitcher.
2. Chill in the refrigerator.
3. Just before serving, add sparkling water or club soda.

*Nutrition (per serving - 1 cup):*
- Calories: 50
- Fat: 0g
- Carbohydrates: 13g
- Fibre: 0g
- Protein: 0g

## NOCHE BUENA TAMALES:

*Ingredients:*
- Tamale dough (see Vegan Tamale Dough recipe)
- 1 cup cooked and seasoned black beans
- 1 cup cooked and seasoned vegetables (bell peppers, zucchini, corn)
- The vegan red or green sauce (see Roasted Tomato Salsa or Salsa Verde recipes)

*Instructions:*
1. Follow the Vegan Tamale Dough recipe to make the dough for the tamales.

2. Put tamales together: Spread tamale dough on corn husks, then add a spoonful of black beans and veggies.
3. Roll the tamales up and steam them for 45–60 minutes or until fully cooked.
4. Serve with a red or green sauce made from plants.

*Nutrition (per tamale):*
- Calories: 300
- Fat: 8g
- Carbohydrates: 50g
- Fiber: 8g
- Protein: 10g

## VEGAN CHRISTMAS POMEGRANATE GUACAMOLE:

*Ingredients:*
- 3 ripe avocados, mashed
- 1/4 cup diced red onion
- 1/4 cup diced tomatoes
- 1/4 cup chopped fresh cilantro
- Juice of 1 lime
- Salt and pepper, to taste
- 1/4 cup pomegranate seeds

*Instructions:*

1. Mix mashed avocados, red onion, tomatoes, chopped cilantro, lime juice, salt, and pepper in a bowl.
2. Gently fold in pomegranate seeds.
3. Serve with tortilla chips.

**Nutrition (per serving - 1/4 cup):**
- Calories: 100
- Fat: 7g
- Carbohydrates: 10g
- Fibre: 5g
- Protein: 2g

## VEGAN CINCO DE MAYO PIÑA COLADA CUPCAKES:

**Ingredients:**
- 1 1/2 cups all-purpose flour
- 1 cup granulated sugar
- 1 teaspoon baking powder
- 1/2 teaspoon baking soda
- 1/4 teaspoon salt
- 1/2 cup canned coconut milk
- 1/2 cup pineapple juice
- 1/4 cup vegetable oil
- 1 teaspoon vanilla extract
- 1 teaspoon white or apple cider vinegar
- Crushed pineapple, drained

- Vegan coconut whipped cream (optional)

***Instructions:***
1. Cupcake liners should line a muffin pan as the oven is preheated to 350°F (175°C).
2. Mix the flour, sugar, salt, baking soda, and baking powder in a bowl.
3. Combine coconut milk, pineapple juice, vegetable oil, vanilla extract, and vinegar in a different bowl.
4. Mix the ingredients—dry and wet—until they are well combined.
5. About two-thirds of the way complete, fill cupcake liners, and bake for 18 to 20 minutes, or until a toothpick inserted in the centre comes out clean.
6. Let them cool fully before icing cupcakes with coconut whipped cream and topping them with crushed pineapple.

***Nutrition (per cupcake):***
- Calories: 200
- Fat: 7g
- Carbohydrates: 32g
- Fibre: 1g
- Protein: 2g

## VEGAN DÍA DE LOS MUERTOS PAN DE MUERTO:

*Ingredients:*

- 4 cups all-purpose flour
- 1/2 cup granulated sugar
- 1 packet of active dry yeast
- 1/2 teaspoon salt
- 1/2 teaspoon ground anise
- 1/2 teaspoon ground cinnamon
- 1/4 teaspoon ground nutmeg
- 1/2 cup nondairy milk (almond, soy, or oat)
- 1/4 cup water
- 1/4 cup vegan butter, melted
- One teaspoon orange zest
- Powdered sugar for dusting

*Instructions:*

1. Mix 2 cups of flour, yeast, salt, ground nutmeg, cinnamon, ground anise, and granulated sugar in a big basin.
2. Lukewarm nondairy milk and water should be heated in a saucepan.
3. Combine the dry ingredients with the warm liquid, vegan butter that has been melted, and orange zest. Mix thoroughly.
4. As you knead the dough, gradually add 2 cups of flour.

5. The dough should rise in a warm location for about an hour or until it has doubled in size, covered with a wet towel.
6. A baking sheet should be lined with parchment paper, and the oven should be preheated to 350°F (175°C).
7. The dough should be pounded into a round loaf with a knob on top (to depict a skull). On the prepared baking sheet, put the bread.
8. For an additional 30 minutes, cover the loaf with a moist cloth and allow it to rise.
9. Bake the bread for 20 to 25 minutes or until golden brown and hollow when tapped on the bottom.
10. Before dusting with confectioners' sugar, allow the pan de muerto to cool.

*Nutrition (per serving - 1 slice, based on 10 pieces):*
- Calories: 220
- Fat: 5g
- Carbohydrates: 38g
- Fibre: 1g
- Protein: 4g

## VEGAN THANKSGIVING ENCHILADAS:

*Ingredients:*
- 8 small corn tortillas

- 2 cups cooked and shredded seitan or jackfruit
- 1 cup diced bell peppers
- 1 cup diced onions
- 1 cup cooked and seasoned black beans
- 1 cup vegan cheese, shredded
- The vegan red or green sauce (see Roasted Tomato Salsa or Salsa Verde recipes)
- Chopped fresh cilantro
- Sliced avocado

**Instructions:**
1. Set the oven's temperature to 375°F (190°C).
2. In a microwave or a dry skillet, reheat the corn tortillas.
3. Sliced bell peppers and onions should be cooked till tender in a skillet.
4. Build the enchiladas: Each tortilla should have a dollop of vegan sauce before being topped with vegan cheese, shredded seitan or jackfruit, sautéed bell peppers and onions, and black beans. The tortillas should be rolled up and put in a baking tray.
5. The enchiladas should be baked for 15 to 20 minutes, or until the cheese is melted and bubbling, with additional sauce on top.
6. Sliced avocado and cilantro should be added as a garnish before serving.

*Nutrition (per serving - 2 enchiladas):*
- Calories: 350
- Fat: 10g
- Carbohydrates: 45g
- Fiber: 10g
- Protein: 15g

## VEGAN HANUKKAH POTATO TACOS WITH VEGAN SOUR CREAM:

*Ingredients:*
- 8 small corn tortillas
- 2 cups cooked and diced potatoes
- 1 cup sauerkraut
- 1/2 cup diced onions
- 1/2 cup chopped fresh dill
- Vegan sour cream (see Vegan Sour Cream recipe)
- Chopped fresh parsley

## Instructions:

1. In a microwave or a dry skillet, reheat the corn tortillas.
2. Combine diced potatoes, sauerkraut, onions, and fresh dill in a bowl.

3. Build the tacos: Put some potato and sauerkraut mixture inside each tortilla.
4. Add chopped parsley and vegan sour cream on top.

*Nutrition (per taco):*
- Calories: 200
- Fat: 5g
- Carbohydrates: 35g
- Fibre: 8g
- Protein: 5g

## VEGAN INDEPENDENCE DAY SALSA FIREWORKS:

*Ingredients:*
- 2 cups diced tomatoes
- 1/2 cup diced red onions
- 1/2 cup diced bell peppers (red, white, and blue colours)
- 1/4 cup chopped fresh cilantro
- Juice of 1 lime
- Salt and pepper, to taste
- Tortilla chips

*Instructions:*

1. Diced tomatoes, red onions, bell peppers, cilantro, lime juice, salt, and pepper should be combined in a bowl with these ingredients.
2. Distribute the salsa along with the tortilla chips on a platter.

*Nutrition (per serving - 1/4 cup salsa with chips):*
- Calories: 50
- Fat: 1g
- Carbohydrates: 10g
- Fiber: 2g
- Protein: 1g

## VEGAN VALENTINE'S DAY CHOCOLATE CHILI TRUFFLES:

*Ingredients:*
- 1 cup vegan dark chocolate, chopped
- 1/4 cup coconut cream
- 1 teaspoon ground chilli powder
- 1/2 teaspoon ground cinnamon
- 1/4 teaspoon vanilla extract
- Cocoa powder or powdered sugar for rolling

*Instructions:*
1. Heat the coconut cream in a microwave-safe bowl until it is warm but not boiling.

2. After adding, melt the vegan dark chocolate that has been chopped.
3. Add vanilla extract, ground cinnamon, and ground chilli powder after stirring until smooth.
4. The mixture should be chilled in the refrigerator until it is manageable.
5. Small truffle balls made of the chocolate mixture should be rolled in either cocoa powder or powdered sugar.
6. Until you're ready to serve, keep the truffles in the refrigerator.

*Nutrition (per truffle, based on 12 truffles):*
- Calories: 70
- Fat: 5g
- Carbohydrates: 6g
- Fibre: 1g
- Protein: 1g

## VEGAN YUCATAN TOFU TACOS:

**Ingredients:**
- 8 small corn tortillas
- 1 block (14 oz) extra-firm tofu, pressed and diced
- 1 tablespoon achiote paste
- Juice of 1 orange

- Juice of 2 limes
- 2 cloves garlic, minced
- 1 teaspoon ground cumin
- Salt and pepper, to taste
- Sliced red onion
- Chopped fresh cilantro
- Sliced radishes
- Lime wedges

**Instructions:**
1. Achiote paste, orange juice, lime juice, minced garlic, ground cumin, salt, and pepper should all be combined in a bowl.
2. Add the marinade to the diced tofu and sit for 30 minutes.
3. Cook heated through and brown in a skillet with marinated tofu.
4. In a microwave or a dry skillet, reheat the corn tortillas.
5. Build the tacos: Each tortilla should be stuffed with sautéed tofu, red onion slices, cilantro, radishes, and lime wedges.

**Nutrition (per serving - 2 tacos):**
- Calories: 250
- Fat: 10g
- Carbohydrates: 30g
- Fibre: 6g

- Protein: 15g

## OAXACAN-STYLE VEGAN MOLE ENCHILADAS:

***Ingredients:***
- 8 small corn tortillas
- 2 cups cooked and shredded seitan or jackfruit
- Vegan mole sauce (see Vegan Mole Poblano recipe)
- Vegan crema (see Vegan Sour Cream with Lime recipe)
- Sesame seeds toasted
- Chopped fresh cilantro

***Instructions:***
1. Set the oven's temperature to 375°F (190°C).
2. In a microwave or a dry skillet, reheat the corn tortillas.
3. Each tortilla should be rolled up after being filled with shredded seitan or jackfruit.
4. Put the enchiladas in a baking dish and cover them with vegan mole sauce.
5. Bake for 15 to 20 minutes or until heated all the way through.

6. Before serving, top with vegan crème, toasted sesame seeds, and cilantro that has been finely chopped.

*Nutrition (per serving - 2 enchiladas):*
- Calories: 300
- Fat: 10g
- Carbohydrates: 40g
- Fiber: 8g
- Protein: 15g

## VEGAN TAMALES DE ELOTE (CORN TAMALES):

*Ingredients:*
- Corn husks soaked in warm water
- 2 cups masa harina (corn flour)
- 1 cup vegetable broth
- 1/2 cup vegan butter or coconut oil, softened
- 1 teaspoon baking powder
- 1 teaspoon salt
- 2 cups fresh corn kernels
- Sliced jalapeños (optional)
- Salsa verde (see Spicy Salsa Verde recipe)
- Vegan crema (see Vegan Sour Cream with Lime recipe)

*Instructions:*
1. Masa harina, softened vegetable broth, vegan butter or coconut oil, baking soda, and salt should all be combined in a bowl until a dough forms.
2. Add the chopped jalapenos and fresh corn if using.
3. Dry a corn husk, then cover it with a thin coating of masa dough.
4. The tamale is sealed by rolling up the corn husk and folding the ends.
5. The tamales should steam for 45 to 60 minutes or until thoroughly done.
6. Serve with vegan crema and green salsa.

*Nutrition (per tamale):*
- Calories: 250
- Fat: 10g
- Carbohydrates: 35g
- Fiber: 4g
- Protein: 5g

## VEGAN CHILES EN NOGADA:

*Ingredients:*
- 4 large poblano peppers, roasted and peeled
- 1 cup cooked and seasoned lentils

- 1/2 cup chopped walnuts
- 1/4 cup diced red onion
- 1/4 cup chopped fresh parsley
- 1/4 cup dried cranberries
- 1/4 teaspoon ground cinnamon
- 1/4 teaspoon ground cloves
- 1/4 teaspoon ground nutmeg
- Vegan walnut cream sauce (see Vegan Walnut Cream Sauce recipe)
- Pomegranate seeds, for garnish

**Instructions:**
1. Set the oven's temperature to 375°F (190°C).
2. Cooked lentils, chopped walnuts, sliced red onion, fresh parsley, dried cranberries, cinnamon, cloves, and nutmeg should all be combined in a bowl.
3. Incorporate the lentil mixture into the roasted poblano peppers.
4. Put the filled peppers in a baking dish and cover them with the vegan walnut cream sauce.
5. Bake for 15 to 20 minutes or until heated all the way through.
6. Before serving, add pomegranate seeds as a garnish.

**Nutrition (per serving - 1 stuffed pepper):**
- Calories: 300

- Fat: 10g
- Carbohydrates: 40g
- Fibre: 10g
- Protein: 15g

## VEGAN COCHINITA PIBIL TACOS:

**Ingredients:**
- 8 small corn tortillas
- 2 cups jackfruit, shredded and cooked in cochinita pibil marinade
- Pickled red onions (see Spicy Pickled Red Onions recipe)
- Chopped fresh cilantro
- Lime wedges

**Instructions:**
1. In a microwave or a dry skillet, reheat the corn tortillas.
2. Each tortilla should be full of shredded jackfruit.
3. Add lime wedges, chopped cilantro, and pickled red onions on top.

**Nutrition (per serving - 2 tacos):**
- Calories: 250
- Fat: 5g
- Carbohydrates: 45g
- Fibre: 8g

- Protein: 10g

## VEGAN ENFRIJOLADAS (BLACK BEAN ENCHILADAS):

*Ingredients:*
- 8 small corn tortillas
- 2 cups cooked and seasoned black beans, mashed
- Vegan black bean sauce (see Spicy Black Beans with Cilantro Lime Rice recipe)
- Chopped fresh cilantro
- Sliced radishes

*Instructions:*
1. In a microwave or a dry skillet, reheat the corn tortillas.
2. Roll up each tortilla after stuffing it with mashed black beans.
3. Arrange the enchiladas and top with vegan black bean sauce on a serving plate.
4. Before serving, garnish with sliced radishes and cilantro.

*Nutrition (per serving - 2 enchiladas):*
- Calories: 300
- Fat: 5g
- Carbohydrates: 45g

- Fiber: 10g
- Protein: 15g

## VEGAN SOPES DE CHORIZO DE SOYA:

*Ingredients:*
- 8 small corn slopes
- 1 cup vegan chorizo de soya, cooked
- Refried beans (see Vegan Refried Beans recipe)
- Sliced avocado
- Chopped fresh cilantro
- Vegan crema (see Vegan Sour Cream with Lime recipe)

*Instructions:*
1. In a microwave or dry skillet, reheat the corn pancakes.
2. Each sope should have a coating of refried beans on it.
3. Add vegan crème, sliced avocado, chopped cilantro, and fried vegan chorizo de soya.

*Nutrition (per serving - 1 sope):*
- Calories: 250
- Fat: 10g
- Carbohydrates: 30g
- Fibre: 6g
- Protein: 10g

## VEGAN CHICHARRÓN EN SALSA VERDE:

*Ingredients:*
- 2 cups cooked and seasoned vegan chicharrón (seitan or tofu), chopped
- Salsa verde (see Spicy Salsa Verde recipe)
- Chopped fresh cilantro
- Lime wedges
- Corn tortillas for serving

*Instructions:*
1. In a skillet or microwave, reheat the chopped vegan chicharrón.
2. In a saucepan, warm the salsa verde.
3. Chicharrón should be served with corn tortillas, salsa verde, chopped cilantro, and lime wedges.

*Nutrition (per serving - 1/2 cup chicharrón with salsa):*
- Calories: 250
- Fat: 10g
- Carbohydrates: 30g
- Fiber: 6g
- Protein: 15g

## VEGAN GUISADO DE NOPALES (CACTUS STEW):

*Ingredients:*
- 2 cups diced nopales (cactus paddles), cooked and drained
- 1 cup diced tomatoes
- 1/2 cup diced onions
- 1/2 cup diced bell peppers
- 2 cloves garlic, minced
- 1 teaspoon ground cumin
- 1 teaspoon ground coriander
- 1/2 teaspoon smoked paprika
- Salt and pepper, to taste
- Chopped fresh cilantro
- Lime wedges
- Corn tortillas for serving

*Instructions:*
1. Tomatoes, diced onions, bell peppers, and chopped garlic are cooked in a skillet until tender.
2. For a few more minutes, add the diced nopales.
3. Add salt, pepper, smoked paprika, ground cumin, and coriander.
4. Along with corn tortillas, lime wedges, and chopped cilantro, serve the guisado de nopales.

*Nutrition (per serving - 1 cup guisado):*
- Calories: 150
- Fat: 1g

- Carbohydrates: 30g
- Fiber: 8g
- Protein: 5g

## VEGAN CHAMORRO DE BORREGO TACOS (LAMB SHANK TACOS):

*Ingredients:*
- 8 small corn tortillas
- 2 cups cooked and seasoned jackfruit or seitan, shredded
- Vegan adobo sauce (see Chipotle Black Bean Soup recipe)
- Sliced red onion
- Chopped fresh cilantro
- Lime wedges

*Instructions:*
1. In a microwave or a dry skillet, reheat the corn tortillas.
2. Each tortilla should be stuffed with seitan or jackfruit shreds.
3. Over the filling, drizzle vegan adobo sauce.
4. Add lime wedges, chopped cilantro, and thinly sliced red onion on top.

*Nutrition (per serving - 2 tacos):*
- Calories: 250

- Fat: 5g
- Carbohydrates: 45g
- Fibre: 8g
- Protein: 10g

## VEGAN MEXICAN SUSHI ROLLS:

***Ingredients:***
- 4 nori sheets
- 2 cups cooked sushi rice, seasoned
- Sliced avocado
- Sliced cucumber
- Sliced bell peppers
- Shredded carrots
- Sliced jalapeños
- Vegan cream cheese
- Soy sauce or tamari for dipping

***Instructions:***
1. Put a bamboo sushi mat on top of a sheet of nori.
2. Over the nori, cover it with a layer of seasoned sushi rice, leaving about 1 inch at the top.
3. Over the rice, scatter the following ingredients: sliced avocado, cucumber, bell peppers, shredded carrots, sliced jalapenos, and vegan cream cheese.

4. Using the bamboo mat, tightly roll the nori, moistening the top edge to seal the roll.
5. Serve the roll with soy sauce or tamari and cut it into bite-sized pieces.

*Nutrition (per serving - 1 roll):*
- Calories: 200
- Fat: 5g
- Carbohydrates: 35g
- Fibre: 5g
- Protein: 5g

## VEGAN MEXICAN-INSPIRED PIZZA:

*Ingredients:*
- 1 prepared pizza crust (store-bought or homemade)
- 1/2 cup vegan refried beans
- 1 cup vegan cheese, shredded
- Sliced bell peppers
- Sliced red onion
- Sliced jalapeños
- Sliced black olives
- Chopped fresh cilantro
- Salsa or hot sauce for drizzling

*Instructions:*
1. As directed for the pizza crust, preheat the oven.

2. Over the pizza dough, spread a layer of vegan refried beans.
3. Over the beans, we grated vegan cheese.
4. Add black olives, red onion, jalapenos, and sliced bell peppers.
5. Pizza should be baked on the crust until the cheese is melted and bubbling.
6. Before serving, garnish with chopped cilantro and a dab of salsa or spicy sauce.

*Nutrition (per serving - 1 slice, based on eight pieces):*
- Calories: 250
- Fat: 10g
- Carbohydrates: 30g
- Fibre: 4g
- Protein: 10g

## TOFU AND VEGETABLE FAJITA STIR-FRY:

*Ingredients:*
- 1 block (14 oz) extra-firm tofu, pressed and sliced
- 2 bell peppers, sliced
- 1 onion, sliced
- 1 tablespoon fajita seasoning
- 2 tablespoons olive oil
- Salt and pepper, to taste

- Sliced avocado
- Chopped fresh cilantro
- Lime wedges
- Tortillas, for serving

***Instructions:***
1. Olive oil is heated over medium-high heat in a skillet.
2. Cook the tofu till golden and crispy after adding it.
3. Add sliced bell peppers and onion to the skillet after moving the tofu to one side.
4. Vegetables should be sautéed till soft after being seasoned with fajita seasoning.
5. Add salt and pepper to taste.
6. With tortillas, sliced avocado, chopped cilantro, lime wedges, and the tofu and veggie fajita stir-fry.

***Nutrition (per serving - 1/4 of the stir-fry, without tortillas):***
- Calories: 250
- Fat: 15g
- Carbohydrates: 20g
- Fibre: 6g
- Protein: 15g

## VEGAN MEXICAN-INSPIRED BUDDHA BOWL:

***Ingredients:***
- Cooked quinoa or rice as the base
- Cooked and seasoned black beans
- Sautéed bell peppers and onions
- Sliced avocado
- Shredded lettuce or greens
- Sliced radishes
- Corn kernels
- Chopped fresh cilantro
- Lime wedges
- Vegan ranchero sauce (see Vegan Ranchero Sauce recipe)

***Instructions:***
1. In a bowl, place cooked quinoa or rice.
2. Add cooked black beans, sautéed bell peppers and onions, sliced avocado, shredded lettuce or greens, thinly sliced radishes, corn kernels, and chopped cilantro as garnishes.
3. Serve with lime wedges and drizzle with vegan ranchero sauce.

***Nutrition (per serving - 1 bowl):***
- Calories: 350
- Fat: 10g
- Carbohydrates: 50g

- Fibre: 10g
- Protein: 15g

## VEGAN MEXICAN-INSPIRED SPRING ROLLS:

*Ingredients:*
- Rice paper wrappers
- Cooked vermicelli rice noodles
- Sliced bell peppers
- Sliced cucumber
- Shredded carrots
- Sliced avocado
- Fresh mint leaves
- Fresh cilantro leaves
- Peanut sauce or hoisin sauce for dipping

*Instructions:*
1. Warm water should be used to make a rice paper wrapper malleable.
2. On the lowest third of the rice paper, arrange a small number of cooked vermicelli rice noodles, sliced bell peppers, cucumber, shredded carrots, sliced avocado, fresh mint leaves, and fresh cilantro leaves.
3. The rice paper is rolled up tightly after folding the sides over the filling.
4. Continue by using the remaining ingredients.

5. Serve the spring rolls with hoisin or peanut sauce on the side.

*Nutrition (per serving - 2 spring rolls):*
- Calories: 200
- Fat: 5g
- Carbohydrates: 35g
- Fibre: 5g
- Protein: 5g

## VEGAN MEXICAN-INSPIRED GRAIN BOWL:

**Ingredients:**
- Cooked grains (quinoa, rice, farro, etc.) as the base
- Cooked and seasoned black beans
- Sautéed bell peppers and onions
- Sliced avocado
- Sliced radishes
- Corn kernels
- Chopped fresh cilantro
- Lime wedges
- Vegan sour cream (see Vegan Sour Cream with Lime recipe)

**Instructions:**
1. In a bowl, arrange the cooked grains.

2. Add corn kernels, chopped cilantro, sautéed bell peppers and onions, sliced avocado, sliced radishes, and cooked black beans on top.
3. Serve with lime wedges and vegan sour cream drizzle.

*Nutrition (per serving - 1 bowl):*
- Calories: 350
- Fat: 10g
- Carbohydrates: 50g
- Fibre: 10g
- Protein: 15g

## VEGAN MEXICAN-INSPIRED TOFU LETTUCE WRAPS:

*Ingredients:*
- Large lettuce leaves (such as iceberg or butter lettuce)
- 1 block (14 oz) extra-firm tofu, pressed and crumbled
- 1 tablespoon taco seasoning
- Sliced bell peppers
- Sliced red onion
- Sliced jalapeños
- Chopped fresh cilantro
- Lime wedges

*Instructions:*
1. Crumble the pressed tofu and heat it thoroughly in a skillet.
2. Mix thoroughly after adding taco spice to the tofu.
3. Put together lettuce wraps: On a plate, place a lettuce leaf and top with tofu that has been crumbled, bell pepper slices, red onion, jalapenos, and cilantro.
4. Wrap the lettuce around the filling, then squeeze some lime juice.

*Nutrition (per serving - 2 lettuce wraps):*
- Calories: 150
- Fat: 5g
- Carbohydrates: 20g
- Fibre: 6g
- Protein: 10g

## JACKFRUIT CARNITAS TOSTADA SALAD:

*Ingredients:*
- 4 small corn tostadas
- 2 cups jackfruit carnitas (cooked in chipotle adobo sauce)
- Shredded lettuce or greens
- Diced tomatoes

- Diced red onion
- Sliced avocado
- Sliced jalapeños
- Chopped fresh cilantro
- Lime wedges

*Instructions:*
1. Place a corn tostada on a plate.
2. Top with jackfruit carnitas, shredded lettuce or greens, diced tomatoes, diced red onion, sliced avocado, sliced jalapeños, and chopped cilantro.
3. Serve with lime wedges.

*Nutrition (per serving - 1 tostada salad):*
- Calories: 250
- Fat: 5g
- Carbohydrates: 40g
- Fibre: 8g
- Protein: 10g

## VEGAN MEXICAN-INSPIRED AVOCADO SUSHI:

*Ingredients:*
- 4 nori sheets
- 2 cups cooked sushi rice, seasoned
- Sliced avocado

- Sliced cucumber
- Sliced bell peppers
- Shredded carrots
- Chopped fresh cilantro
- Lime wedges
- Soy sauce or tamari for dipping

***Instructions:***
1. Put a bamboo sushi mat on top of a sheet of nori.
2. Over the nori, cover it with a layer of seasoned sushi rice, leaving about 1 inch at the top.
3. Over the rice, spread out the sliced avocado, cucumber, bell peppers, shredded carrots, cilantro, and a squeeze of lime juice.
4. Using the bamboo mat, tightly roll the nori, moistening the top edge to seal the roll.
5. Serve the roll with soy sauce or tamari and cut it into bite-sized pieces.

***Nutrition (per serving - 1 roll):***
- Calories: 200
- Fat: 5g
- Carbohydrates: 35g
- Fibre: 5g
- Protein: 5g

## MEXICAN-INSPIRED VEGAN RAMEN:

*Ingredients:*
- 2 packs of vegan ramen noodles
- Vegan ramen broth (see Vegan Tortilla Soup recipe)
- Sautéed bell peppers and onions
- Sliced avocado
- Chopped fresh cilantro
- Lime wedges
- Sliced jalapeños

*Instructions:*
1. The vegan ramen noodles should be prepared as directed on the package and then drained.
2. In a saucepan, warm the vegan ramen broth.
3. Put together ramen bowls: Divide the cooked ramen noodles between the bowls, then top with the sautéed bell peppers, onions, avocado, cilantro, and jalapenos.
4. Over the toppings, pour the boiling vegan ramen broth.
5. Slices of lime are optional.

*Nutrition (per serving - 1 bowl):*
- Calories: 350
- Fat: 10g
- Carbohydrates: 50g
- Fibre: 6g
- Protein: 10g

## VEGAN MEXICAN MAC AND CHEESE:

*Ingredients:*
- 8 oz vegan macaroni or pasta, cooked
- 1 cup cooked and seasoned black beans
- Vegan cheese sauce (see Vegan Queso Fundido recipe)
- Sliced jalapeños (optional)
- Chopped fresh cilantro

*Instructions:*
1. Combine cooked macaroni or pasta, cooked black beans, and vegan cheese sauce in a large bowl.
2. Mix well to coat the pasta with the cheese sauce.
3. Serve the vegan Mexican mac and cheese with sliced jalapeños and chopped cilantro.

*Nutrition (per serving - 1 cup):*
- Calories: 300
- Fat: 10g
- Carbohydrates: 40g
- Fibre: 8g
- Protein: 10g

## VEGAN MEXICAN-INSPIRED SHEPHERD'S PIE:

*Ingredients:*
- 4 cups cooked and seasoned lentils
- Sautéed bell peppers and onions
- Mashed sweet potatoes or mashed cauliflower
- Vegan queso fresco (see Vegan Queso Fundido recipe)
- Chopped fresh cilantro

*Instructions:*
1. Set the oven's temperature to 375°F (190°C).
2. Layer cooked lentils, sautéed bell peppers, onions, and mashed sweet potatoes or cauliflower in a baking dish.
3. Top with a sprinkle of vegan queso fresco.
4. Bake for 20 to 25 minutes or until the top is golden and the food is thoroughly heated.
5. Before serving, garnish with chopped cilantro.

*Nutrition (per serving - 1/4 of the shepherd's pie):*
- Calories: 300
- Fat: 5g
- Carbohydrates: 50g
- Fibre: 10g
- Protein: 15g

## VEGAN MEXICAN CHILI CHEESE FRIES:

*Ingredients:*
- Baked or oven-fried french fries
- Vegan chilli (see Mexican Quinoa Chili recipe)
- Vegan cheese sauce (see Vegan Queso Fundido recipe)
- Sliced jalapeños (optional)
- Chopped fresh cilantro

*Instructions:*
1. Arrange baked or oven-fried french fries on a serving plate.
2. Pour vegan chilli over the fries.
3. Drizzle vegan cheese sauce over the chilli.
4. Top with sliced jalapeños and chopped cilantro.

*Nutrition (per serving - 1 plate):*
- Calories: 400
- Fat: 10g
- Carbohydrates: 60g
- Fibre: 10g
- Protein: 15g

## VEGAN MEXICAN-INSPIRED STUFFED PEPPERS:

*Ingredients:*
- 4 bell peppers, halved and seeds removed

- 2 cups cooked and seasoned quinoa or rice
- 1 cup cooked and seasoned black beans
- Sliced avocado
- Chopped fresh cilantro
- Vegan sour cream (see Vegan Sour Cream with Lime recipe)

*Instructions:*
1. Set the oven's temperature to 375°F (190°C).
2. Put the halves of the bell pepper in a baking dish.
3. Black beans and cooked quinoa or rice should be placed inside each pepper half.
4. Bake the peppers for 20 to 25 minutes or until they are soft.
5. With sliced avocado, chopped cilantro, and vegan sour cream on the side, serve the stuffed peppers.

*Nutrition (per serving - 1 stuffed pepper half):*
- Calories: 250
- Fat: 5g
- Carbohydrates: 40g
- Fibre: 8g
- Protein: 10g

## VEGAN MEXICAN-INSPIRED LASAGNA:

### Ingredients:
- 9 lasagna noodles, cooked
- Vegan tofu ricotta (see Tofu and Vegetable Enchiladas recipe)
- Sautéed bell peppers and onions
- Vegan mole sauce (see Vegan Mole Poblano recipe)
- Vegan queso fresco (see Vegan Queso Fundido recipe)
- Chopped fresh cilantro

### Instructions:
1. Set the oven's temperature to 375°F (190°C).
2. Prepared lasagna noodles, vegan tofu ricotta, sautéed bell peppers, onions, and vegan mole sauce are placed in a baking dish.
3. Till all the ingredients are utilized, keep layering.
4. Top with a sprinkle of vegan queso fresco.
5. Bake for about 25 to 30 minutes or until bubbling and well cooked.
6. Before serving, garnish with chopped cilantro.

### Nutrition (per serving - 1/6 of the lasagna):
- Calories: 350
- Fat: 10g
- Carbohydrates: 50g
- Fibre: 8g
- Protein: 15g

## VEGAN MEXICAN-INSPIRED GOULASH:

*Ingredients:*
- 2 cups cooked and seasoned lentils
- Sautéed bell peppers and onions
- Cooked macaroni or pasta
- Vegan cheese sauce (see Vegan Queso Fundido recipe)
- Chopped fresh cilantro

*Instructions:*
1. Combine cooked lentils, bell peppers, onions, and macaroni or pasta in a big bowl.
2. All ingredients should be thoroughly combined.
3. Goulash should be coated with vegan cheese sauce.
4. Before serving, garnish with chopped cilantro.

*Nutrition (per serving - 1 cup):*
- Calories: 300
- Fat: 5g
- Carbohydrates: 50g
- Fibre: 10g
- Protein: 15g

## VEGAN MEXICAN-INSPIRED BISCUITS AND GRAVY:

*Ingredients:*
- Vegan biscuits (store-bought or homemade)
- Vegan gravy (see Creamy Chipotle Sauce recipe)
- Sautéed bell peppers and onions
- Chopped fresh cilantro

*Instructions:*
1. Split the vegan biscuits in half and place them on a plate.
2. Pour warm vegan gravy over the biscuits.
3. Top with sautéed bell peppers and onions.
4. Garnish with chopped cilantro before serving.

*Nutrition (per serving - 2 biscuits with gravy):*
- Calories: 300
- Fat: 10g
- Carbohydrates: 40g
- Fibre: 6g
- Protein: 10g

## VEGAN MEXICAN-INSPIRED MEATLOAF:

*Ingredients:*

- 2 cups cooked and seasoned lentils
- 1 cup breadcrumbs (gluten-free, if needed)
- Sautéed bell peppers and onions
- Vegan barbecue sauce
- Chopped fresh cilantro

*Instructions:*
1. Set the oven's temperature to 375°F (190°C).
2. Cooked lentils, breadcrumbs, sautéed bell peppers, and onions should all be combined in a big bowl.
3. In a loaf pan, press the lentil mixture down.
4. Over the top, apply a layer of vegan barbeque sauce.
5. Bake for about 25 to 30 minutes or until well heated, and the top is just beginning to crisp.
6. Before serving, garnish with chopped cilantro.

*Nutrition (per serving - 1/6 of the meatloaf):*
- Calories: 300
- Fat: 5g
- Carbohydrates: 50g
- Fibre: 10g
- Protein: 15g

## VEGAN MEXICAN-INSPIRED POT PIE:

*Ingredients:*
- 2 cups cooked and seasoned lentils

- Sautéed bell peppers and onions
- Vegan pot pie filling (see Vegan Mushroom and Spinach Enchiladas recipe)
- Vegan pie crust (store-bought or homemade)
- Chopped fresh cilantro

**Instructions:**
1. As directed by the pie crust, preheat the oven.
2. Lentils cooked, bell peppers, onions, and vegan pot pie filling should all be combined on a pie plate.
3. The vegan pie crust should be rolled out and put on the filling.
4. Trim and crimp the crust's edges.
5. To let steam out, make a few slits in the crust.
6. Bake the pie as directed on the pie crust until the filling is bubbling and the crust is golden.
7. Before serving, garnish with chopped cilantro.

*Nutrition (per serving - 1/6 of the pot pie):*
- Calories: 350
- Fat: 10g
- Carbohydrates: 45g
- Fibre: 8g
- Protein: 15g

## VEGAN MEXICAN-INSPIRED BREAKFAST CASSEROLE:

*Ingredients:*
- 2 cups cooked and seasoned black beans
- Sautéed bell peppers and onions
- Cubed and seasoned tofu (see Tofu Scramble Breakfast Tacos recipe)
- Vegan cheese shreds
- 1 cup plant-based milk
- 1/4 cup nutritional yeast
- 1 tablespoon ground flaxseed
- 1 teaspoon ground cumin
- Salt and pepper, to taste
- Chopped fresh cilantro

*Instructions:*
1. Set the oven's temperature to 375°F (190°C).
2. In a baking dish, layer cubed and spiced tofu, cooked black beans, sautéed bell peppers and onions, and vegan cheese shreds.
3. Mix plant-based milk, nutritional yeast, flaxseed, cumin, ground, salt, and pepper in a basin.
4. Over the casserole, pour the milk mixture.
5. Bake for approximately 25 to 30 minutes or until well heated; the top is brown.
6. Before serving, garnish with chopped cilantro.

*Nutrition (per serving - 1/6 of the casserole):*
- Calories: 350
- Fat: 10g
- Carbohydrates: 40g
- Fibre: 10g
- Protein: 20g

## VEGAN GRILLED PORTOBELLO FAJITAS:

*Ingredients:*
- 4 large portobello mushrooms, cleaned and stems removed
- Sliced bell peppers and onions
- Fajita marinade (see Tofu and Vegetable Fajita Stir-Fry recipe)
- Sliced avocado
- Chopped fresh cilantro
- Lime wedges
- Tortillas, for serving

*Instructions:*
1. For around 30 minutes, marinate portobello mushrooms in the fajita marinade in a bowl.
2. A grill or grill pan should be preheated to high heat.

3. Sliced bell peppers, onions, and portobello mushrooms should be grilled until soft and slightly browned.
4. The grilled portobello mushrooms into slices.
5. Build the fajitas: Place sautéed bell peppers, onions, and grilled portobello mushrooms in slices on a tortilla.
6. Avocado slices, chopped cilantro, and a squeeze of lime juice go on top.

***Nutrition (per serving - 2 fajitas):***
- Calories: 250
- Fat: 5g
- Carbohydrates: 45g
- Fiber: 8g
- Protein: 10g

## VEGAN MEXICAN-INSPIRED GRILLED VEGGIE PLATTER:

***Ingredients:***
- Assorted vegetables (bell peppers, onions, zucchini, etc.)
- Grilled vegetable marinade (see Grilled Veggie Fajitas recipe)
- Sliced avocado
- Chopped fresh cilantro
- Lime wedges

*Instructions:*
1. Mixtures of veggies should be marinated in the grilled vegetable marinade for around 30 minutes.
2. A grill or grill pan should be preheated to high heat.
3. Grill the vegetables with the marinade until they are soft and slightly browned.
4. The grilled vegetables should be arranged on a serving plate.
5. Avocado slices, cilantro, and lime wedges should be added as a garnish.

*Nutrition (per serving - 1/4 of the platter):*
- Calories: 150
- Fat: 5g
- Carbohydrates: 25g
- Fibre: 8g
- Protein: 5g

## VEGAN MEXICAN-INSPIRED BBQ SKEWERS:

*Ingredients:*
- Assorted vegetables (bell peppers, onions, mushrooms, etc.)
- Vegan barbecue sauce
- Sliced avocado

- Chopped fresh cilantro
- Lime wedges

***Instructions:***
1. Put a variety of vegetables on skewers.
2. Vegetables on skewers should be covered in vegan barbeque sauce.
3. A grill or grill pan should be preheated to high heat.
4. Vegetables on the skewers should be cooked through and slightly browned during grilling.
5. Sliced avocado, chopped cilantro, and lime wedges should be served with the BBQ skewers.

***Nutrition (per serving - 2 skewers):***
- Calories: 150
- Fat: 5g
- Carbohydrates: 25g
- Fibre: 8g
- Protein: 5g

## GRILLED TOFU TACOS WITH PINEAPPLE SALSA:

***Ingredients:***
- 8 small corn tortillas

- Grilled tofu slices (marinated in a Mexican-inspired marinade)
- Pineapple salsa (see Pineapple Salsa recipe)
- Sliced avocado
- Chopped fresh cilantro
- Lime wedges

*Instructions:*
1. Warm the corn tortillas in a dry skillet or microwave.
2. Fill each tortilla with grilled tofu slices.
3. Top with pineapple salsa, sliced avocado, chopped cilantro, and a squeeze of lime juice.

*Nutrition (per serving - 2 tacos):*
- Calories: 250
- Fat: 5g
- Carbohydrates: 40g
- Fibre: 8g
- Protein: 10g

## VEGAN MEXICAN-INSPIRED BBQ JACKFRUIT SANDWICHES:

*Ingredients:*
- 4 whole wheat or gluten-free buns
- BBQ jackfruit (cooked in barbecue sauce)

- Sliced red onion
- Sliced pickles
- Vegan coleslaw (see Vegan Coleslaw recipe)
- Sliced avocado
- Chopped fresh cilantro

*Instructions:*
1. Split the buns and toast them if desired.
2. Fill each bun with BBQ jackfruit.
3. Top with sliced red onion, pickles, vegan coleslaw, sliced avocado, and chopped cilantro.

*Nutrition (per serving - 1 sandwich):*
- Calories: 300
- Fat: 5g
- Carbohydrates: 50g
- Fibre: 10g
- Protein: 10g

## VEGAN MEXICAN-INSPIRED PEANUT BUTTER AND JELLY TORTILLAS:

*Ingredients:*
- 2 whole wheat or gluten-free tortillas
- Peanut butter
- Fruit preserves (such as strawberry or grape)
- Sliced banana

*Instructions:*
1. Spread fruit preserves on one tortilla, then peanut butter on the other.
2. Stack the banana slices on one side.
3. To make a sandwich, press the two tortillas together.
4. Serve after cutting into wedges.

*Nutrition (per serving - 1 tortilla sandwich):*
- Calories: 300
- Fat: 10g
- Carbohydrates: 45g
- Fibre: 6g
- Protein: 8g

## VEGAN MEXICAN-INSPIRED ANTS ON A LOG:

*Ingredients:*
- Celery sticks
- Peanut butter
- Raisins

*Instructions:*
1. Spread peanut butter inside the celery sticks.
2. Place raisins on top of the peanut butter.

*Nutrition (per serving - 2 celery sticks):*

- Calories: 100
- Fat: 5g
- Carbohydrates: 10g
- Fibre: 3g
- Protein: 3g

## VEGAN MEXICAN-INSPIRED GRILLED "CHEESE" QUESADILLA:

*Ingredients:*
- 2 whole wheat or gluten-free tortillas
- Vegan cheese shreds
- Sliced bell peppers
- Sliced red onion
- Sliced avocado

*Instructions:*
1. One tortilla should be placed on a medium-hot grill.
2. Shreds of vegan cheese should be sprinkled on half the tortilla.
3. Add sliced bell peppers, red onion, and avocado on top.
4. Cook the tortilla until both sides are crisp by folding it in half.

**Nutrition (per serving - 1 quesadilla):**

- Calories: 350
- Fat: 15g
- Carbohydrates: 45g
- Fiber: 8g
- Protein: 10g

## VEGAN MEXICAN-INSPIRED CAULIFLOWER "WINGS":

***Ingredients:***
- 1 small head of cauliflower, cut into florets
- Vegan buffalo wing sauce
- Vegan ranch dressing (see Creamy Chipotle Sauce recipe)
- Chopped fresh cilantro

***Instructions:***
1. A baking sheet should be lined with parchment paper, and the oven should be preheated to 425°F (220°C).
2. Sprinkle vegan buffalo wing sauce over cauliflower florets.
3. On the baking sheet, arrange the cauliflower and bake for 20 to 25 minutes or until crispy.
4. Garnish with chopped cilantro and vegan ranch dressing.

**Nutrition (per serving - 1 cup of cauliflower "wings"):**
- Calories: 150
- Fat: 5g
- Carbohydrates: 20g
- Fibre: 6g
- Protein: 5g

**Vegan Mexican-Inspired Sloppy Joes:**

**Ingredients:**
- 1 cup cooked and seasoned lentils
- Sautéed bell peppers and onions
- Vegan barbecue sauce
- Whole wheat or gluten-free buns

**Instructions:**
1. Cooked lentils, sautéed bell peppers, and onions should be combined in a bowl.
2. Combine it with vegan barbeque sauce depending on how saucy you like.
3. Fill the buns with the lentil mixture after warming them up.

**Nutrition (per serving - 1 sandwich):**
- Calories: 300
- Fat: 5g
- Carbohydrates: 50g
- Fibre: 10g
- Protein: 15g

## VEGAN MEXICAN-INSPIRED TOFU DINO NUGGETS:

*Ingredients:*
- 1 block of firm tofu, pressed and cut into dino nugget shapes
- Mexican-inspired seasoning (chilli powder, cumin, paprika, garlic powder, onion powder, salt)
- Breadcrumbs (gluten-free, if needed)
- Dipping sauce of your choice

*Instructions:*
1. Bake at 375°F (190°C) for 15 minutes with a baking sheet lined with parchment paper.
2. Tofu dinosaur nuggets should be breaded and seasoned in a Mexican-inspired manner.
3. Spread the coated tofu nuggets on a baking sheet and bake for 20 to 25 minutes or until crispy.
4. Serve with the dipping sauce of your choice.

*Nutrition (per serving - 1/2 cup of tofu nuggets):*
- Calories: 200
- Fat: 8g
- Carbohydrates: 20g
- Fibre: 4g

- Protein: 15g

## VEGAN MEXICAN-INSPIRED MACARONI SALAD:

*Ingredients:*
- 2 cups cooked macaroni or pasta
- Vegan mayo
- Diced bell peppers
- Diced red onion
- Diced cucumber
- Chopped fresh cilantro
- Lime juice
- Mexican-inspired seasoning (chilli powder, cumin, paprika, garlic powder, onion powder, salt)

*Instructions:*
1. In a bowl, combine cooked macaroni, diced bell peppers, red onion, cucumber, chopped cilantro, and a squeeze of lime juice.
2. Mix in vegan mayo and Mexican-inspired seasoning to taste.
3. Refrigerate before serving.

**Nutrition (per serving - 1 cup):**

- Calories: 300
- Fat: 10g
- Carbohydrates: 40g
- Fibre: 4g
- Protein: 8g

## VEGAN MEXICAN-INSPIRED PIZZA BAGELS:

*Ingredients:*
- 2 whole wheat or gluten-free bagels, sliced
- Vegan pizza sauce
- Vegan cheese shreds
- Sliced bell peppers
- Sliced red onion
- Sliced black olives
- Sliced jalapeños

*Instructions:*
1. Bake at 375°F (190°C) for 15 minutes with a baking sheet lined with parchment paper.
2. On the baking sheet, arrange the bagel slices.
3. Each bagel piece should be covered in vegan pizza sauce.
4. Add vegan cheese crumbles, bell pepper, red onion, black olives, and jalapenos.
5. Bake the dish for 10 to 15 minutes or until the cheese bubbles and melts.

*Nutrition (per serving - 1 pizza bagel):*
- Calories: 250
- Fat: 8g
- Carbohydrates: 35g
- Fibre: 6g
- Protein: 10g

## VEGAN MEXICAN-INSPIRED FRUIT ROLL-UPS:

*Ingredients:*
- Assorted fresh fruits (strawberries, mango, kiwi, etc.)
- Agave syrup or maple syrup
- Lime juice

*Instructions:*
1. Blend fresh fruits with lime juice, agave syrup, or maple syrup.
2. On a baking sheet covered with parchment paper, spread the fruit puree.
3. Dehydrate the fruit in the oven for 4-6 hours at the lowest temperature (about 170°F or 75°C) or until it is no longer sticky.
4. Roll up the fruit roll-up after cutting it into strips.

**Nutrition (per serving - 1 roll-up):**
- Calories: 50
- Fat: 0g
- Carbohydrates: 12g
- Fiber: 2g
- Protein: 0g

## VEGAN MEXICAN-INSPIRED POTATO SMILEYS:

**Ingredients:**
- Potatoes peeled and cooked
- Mexican-inspired seasoning (chilli powder, cumin, paprika, garlic powder, onion powder, salt)
- Vegan sour cream
- Sliced black olives
- Chopped fresh cilantro

**Instructions:**
1. Cooked potatoes are mashed with seasoning with a Mexican flavour.
2. Make smiling faces out of the mashed potatoes.

3. The potato smileys should be baked for 15 to 20 minutes at 375°F (190°C) or until they begin to get somewhat crispy.
4. Serve with a garnish of chopped cilantro, black olive slices, and vegan sour cream.

*Nutrition (per serving - 4 potato smileys):*
- Calories: 200
- Fat: 2g
- Carbohydrates: 40g
- Fibre: 6g
- Protein: 5g

## VEGAN MEXICAN-INSPIRED ZUCCHINI NOODLES WITH PICO DE GALLO:

*Ingredients:*
- 2 medium zucchinis, spiralized into noodles
- Pico de gallo (see Pico de Gallo recipe)
- Sliced avocado
- Chopped fresh cilantro
- Lime wedges

*Instructions:*
1. In a bowl, toss zucchini noodles with pico de gallo.

2. Serve with sliced avocado, chopped cilantro, and lime wedges.

**Nutrition (per serving - 1 cup of zucchini noodles):**
- Calories: 100
- Fat: 5g
- Carbohydrates: 15g
- Fibre: 4g
- Protein: 3g

## VEGAN MEXICAN-INSPIRED STUFFED BELL PEPPERS WITH QUINOA:

**Ingredients:**
- 4 bell peppers, tops removed and seeds removed
- Quinoa, cooked and seasoned
- Sautéed bell peppers and onions
- Black beans, cooked and seasoned
- Vegan cheese shreds
- Chopped fresh cilantro

**Instructions:**
1. An oven-safe baking dish should be lightly greased and heated to 375°F (190°C).
2. Combine cooked quinoa, bell peppers, onions, and black beans in a bowl.

3. Stuff the quinoa mixture inside each bell pepper.
4. Over the packed peppers, scatter vegan cheese slivers.
5. The stuffed peppers should be baked for 20 to 25 minutes or until soft.
6. Before serving, garnish with chopped cilantro.

*Nutrition (per serving - 1 stuffed pepper):*
- Calories: 250
- Fat: 5g
- Carbohydrates: 40g
- Fibre: 8g
- Protein: 10g

## VEGAN MEXICAN-INSPIRED AVOCADO AND BLACK BEAN SALAD:

*Ingredients:*
- Diced avocado
- Black beans, cooked and seasoned
- Diced bell peppers
- Diced red onion
- Diced cucumber
- Chopped fresh cilantro
- Lime juice

- Mexican-inspired seasoning (chilli powder, cumin, paprika, garlic powder, onion powder, salt)

*Instructions:*
1. Diced avocado, black beans, bell peppers, red onion, cucumber, cilantro, and a squeeze of lime juice should all be combined in a bowl.
2. Add to taste the Mexican-inspired seasoning mixture.
3. Before serving, chill.

*Nutrition (per serving - 1 cup):*
- Calories: 250
- Fat: 10g
- Carbohydrates: 35g
- Fiber: 12g
- Protein: 10g

## VEGAN MEXICAN-INSPIRED CUCUMBER AND WATERMELON SALAD:

*Ingredients:*
- Diced cucumber
- Diced watermelon
- Sliced red onion
- Chopped fresh cilantro

- Lime juice
- Tajin seasoning (chilli-lime seasoning)

*Instructions:*
1. Cucumber, watermelon, red onion, and cilantro are diced and combined in a bowl.
2. Sprinkle Tajin spice and lime juice over the salad.
3. Gently blend by tossing.

*Nutrition (per serving - 1 cup):*
- Calories: 50
- Fat: 0g
- Carbohydrates: 12g
- Fibre: 1g
- Protein: 1g

## VEGAN MEXICAN-INSPIRED CHIA SEED PUDDING WITH MANGO:

*Ingredients:*
- Chia seeds
- Almond milk or coconut milk
- Mango chunks
- Agave syrup or maple syrup
- Mexican-inspired seasoning (chilli powder, cumin, paprika, cinnamon)

*Instructions:*

1. Chia seeds and almond or coconut milk should be combined in a jar. Stir thoroughly, then chill for the night.
2. Layer mango chunks and chia seed pudding in the morning.
3. Add some seasoning with a Mexican flair and drizzle with agave or maple syrup.

***Nutrition (per serving - 1 cup):***
- Calories: 200
- Fat: 7g
- Carbohydrates: 30g
- Fibre: 10g
- Protein: 5

## VEGAN MEXICAN-INSPIRED GREEN SMOOTHIE BOWL:

***Ingredients:***
- Spinach or kale
- Frozen banana
- Frozen mango chunks
- Almond milk or coconut milk
- Chopped fresh cilantro
- Toppings: Sliced kiwi, chia seeds, pumpkin seeds

***Instructions:***

1. Blend spinach or kale, frozen banana, frozen mango chunks, and almond or coconut milk until smooth.
2. Pour into a bowl and top with sliced kiwi, chia seeds, pumpkin seeds, and chopped cilantro.

*Nutrition (per serving - 1 smoothie bowl):*
- Calories: 300
- Fat: 10g
- Carbohydrates: 45g
- Fibre: 10g
- Protein: 5g

## VEGAN MEXICAN-INSPIRED BLACK BEAN AND CORN QUINOA SALAD:

*Ingredients:*
- Cooked quinoa
- Black beans, cooked and seasoned
- Corn kernels, cooked
- Diced bell peppers
- Diced red onion
- Chopped fresh cilantro
- Lime juice
- Mexican-inspired seasoning (chilli powder, cumin, paprika, garlic powder, onion powder, salt)

*Instructions:*
1. Combine cooked quinoa, black beans, corn kernels, bell peppers, red onion, and chopped cilantro in a bowl.
2. Drizzle with lime juice and sprinkle Mexican-inspired seasoning over the salad.
3. Toss gently to combine.

*Nutrition (per serving - 1 cup):*
- Calories: 250
- Fat: 5g
- Carbohydrates: 40g
- Fibre: 8g
- Protein: 10g

## VEGAN MEXICAN-INSPIRED CHICKPEA SALAD WITH CUMIN DRESSING:

**Ingredients:**
- Cooked chickpeas
- Diced cucumber
- Diced red onion
- Chopped fresh cilantro
- Lime juice
- Cumin dressing (cumin, olive oil, lime juice, agave syrup or maple syrup)

*Instructions:*

1. Combine cooked chickpeas, diced cucumber, red onion, and chopped cilantro in a bowl.
2. Drizzle with lime juice and toss with cumin dressing.

*Nutrition (per serving - 1 cup):*
- Calories: 250
- Fat: 10g
- Carbohydrates: 35g
- Fibre: 8g
- Protein: 10g

## VEGAN MEXICAN-INSPIRED CAULIFLOWER RICE BOWL:

*Ingredients:*
- Cauliflower rice, cooked
- Sautéed bell peppers and onions
- Black beans, cooked and seasoned
- Sliced avocado
- Chopped fresh cilantro
- Lime wedges
- Mexican-inspired seasoning (chilli powder, cumin, paprika, garlic powder, onion powder, salt)

*Instructions:*

1. Cauliflower rice that has been cooked, bell peppers, onions, and black beans should all be combined in a bowl.
2. Mix thoroughly after adding a Mexican-inspired flavour.
3. Avocado slices, cilantro, and lime wedges should be added as a garnish.

*Nutrition (per serving - 1 bowl):*
- Calories: 200
- Fat: 8g
- Carbohydrates: 30g
- Fiber: 12g
- Protein: 10g

## VEGAN MEXICAN-INSPIRED GRILLED VEGGIE WRAP:

*Ingredients:*
- Whole wheat or gluten-free tortilla
- Grilled vegetables (assorted bell peppers, onions, zucchini, etc.)
- Sliced avocado
- Vegan chipotle mayo (see Creamy Chipotle Sauce recipe)
- Chopped fresh cilantro

*Instructions:*

1. On one half of a tortilla, spread out grilled vegetables.
2. Add vegan chipotle mayo, chopped cilantro, and avocado slices on top.
3. The tortilla should be rolled into a wrap.

*Nutrition (per serving - 1 wrap):*
- Calories: 250
- Fat: 10g
- Carbohydrates: 35g
- Fibre: 8g
- Protein: 5g

## VEGAN MEXICAN-INSPIRED ONE-POT RICE AND BEANS:

*Ingredients:*
- Cooked rice
- Cooked and seasoned black beans
- Sautéed bell peppers and onions
- Mexican-inspired seasoning (chilli powder, cumin, paprika, garlic powder, onion powder, salt)
- Chopped fresh cilantro
- Lime wedges

*Instructions:*

1. Combine cooked rice, seasoned black beans, sautéed bell peppers and onions, and Mexican-inspired seasoning in a large pot.
2. Mix well and heat over low heat until heated through.
3. Serve with chopped cilantro and lime wedges.

*Nutrition (per serving - 1 cup):*
- Calories: 250
- Fat: 5g
- Carbohydrates: 40g
- Fibre: 8g
- Protein: 10g

## VEGAN MEXICAN-INSPIRED SHEET PAN FAJITAS:

*Ingredients:*
- Sliced bell peppers and onions
- Sliced portobello mushrooms (optional)
- Mexican-inspired fajita marinade (see Tofu and Vegetable Fajita Stir-Fry recipe)
- Whole wheat or gluten-free tortillas
- Sliced avocado
- Chopped fresh cilantro
- Lime wedges

*Instructions:*
1. A baking sheet should be lined with parchment paper, and the oven should be preheated to 425°F (220°C).
2. Add sliced bell peppers, onions, and, if using, mushrooms to the fajita marinade.
3. Spread the vegetables and roast on a baking sheet for 20 to 25 minutes or until tender.
4. Fill warm tortillas with roasted vegetable filling.
5. Avocado slices, cilantro, and lime wedges should be added as a garnish.

*Nutrition (per serving - 2 fajitas):*
- Calories: 300
- Fat: 8g
- Carbohydrates: 45g
- Fiber: 10g
- Protein: 10g

## VEGAN MEXICAN-INSPIRED 15-MINUTE SALSA PASTA:

*Ingredients:*
- Cooked pasta (such as penne or rotini)
- Fresh salsa (see Spicy Salsa Verde recipe)
- Sautéed bell peppers and onions
- Black beans, cooked and seasoned
- Chopped fresh cilantro

- Lime wedges

*Instructions:*
1. Cooked pasta, fresh salsa, sautéed bell peppers, onions, and seasoned black beans should all be combined in a sizable pan.
2. Cook until well cooked over medium heat.
3. Serve with lime wedges and chopped cilantro.

*Nutrition (per serving - 1 cup):*
- Calories: 250
- Fat: 5g
- Carbohydrates: 40g
- Fibre: 8g
- Protein: 10g

## VEGAN MEXICAN-INSPIRED TOFU TACOS IN A HURRY:

*Ingredients:*
- Cooked and seasoned tofu cubes
- Whole wheat or gluten-free tortillas
- Shredded lettuce
- Diced tomatoes
- Diced red onion
- Sliced avocado
- Chopped fresh cilantro
- Lime wedges

**Instructions:**

1. Cubes of cooked, seasoned tofu should be warmed.
2. Tofu cubes, tomatoes, red onion, sliced avocado, and cilantro are all added to the tortillas.
3. Slices of lime are optional.

*Nutrition (per serving - 2 tacos):*
- Calories: 250
- Fat: 10g
- Carbohydrates: 30g
- Fibre: 8g
- Protein: 10g

## VEGAN MEXICAN-INSPIRED QUICK GUACAMOLE TOAST:

*Ingredients:*
- Whole wheat or gluten-free bread, toasted
- Mashed avocado
- Diced tomatoes
- Diced red onion
- Chopped fresh cilantro
- Lime juice

- Mexican-inspired seasoning (chilli powder, cumin, paprika, garlic powder, onion powder, salt)

*Instructions:*
1. Toast the bread, then top with mashed avocado.
2. Add diced tomatoes, red onion, cilantro, and a squeeze of lime juice as a garnish.
3. Season with a bit of spice with a Mexican flair.

*Nutrition (per serving - 1 slice of toast):*
- Calories: 150
- Fat: 7g
- Carbohydrates: 20g
- Fibre: 6g
- Protein: 3g

## VEGAN MEXICAN-INSPIRED INSTANT POT CHILI:

**Ingredients:**
- Cooked and seasoned black beans
- Cooked and seasoned kidney beans
- Sautéed bell peppers and onions
- Diced tomatoes
- Vegetable broth

- Mexican-inspired seasoning (chilli powder, cumin, paprika, garlic powder, onion powder, salt)
- Chopped fresh cilantro
- Lime wedges

*Instructions:*
1. Cooked black beans, cooked kidney beans, sautéed bell peppers and onions, diced tomatoes, vegetable broth, and Mexican seasoning are all combined in an Instant Pot.
2. Cook for a few minutes under pressure or on the chilli setting.
3. Serve with lime wedges and chopped cilantro.

*Nutrition (per serving - 1 cup):*
- Calories: 200
- Fat: 5g
- Carbohydrates: 30g
- Fibre: 10g
- Protein: 10g

## VEGAN MEXICAN-INSPIRED 10-MINUTE TACO SALAD:

*Ingredients:*
- Cooked and seasoned lentils or black beans
- Shredded lettuce

- Diced tomatoes
- Diced red onion
- Sliced black olives
- Vegan cheese shreds
- Tortilla chips, crushed
- Vegan ranch dressing (see Creamy Chipotle Sauce recipe)
- Chopped fresh cilantro
- Lime wedges

***Instructions:***
1. Cooked black beans or lentils, diced tomatoes, red onion, black olives, and vegan cheese shreds should all be combined in a bowl.
2. Add some crumbled tortilla chips and vegan ranch dressing over the top.
3. Lime wedges and cilantro cut for garnish.

***Nutrition (per serving - 1 bowl):***
- Calories: 300
- Fat: 10g
- Carbohydrates: 40g
- Fiber: 12g
- Protein: 15g

***Vegan Mexican-Inspired Microwave Nachos:***
***Ingredients:***
- Tortilla chips

- Vegan cheese shreds
- Cooked and seasoned black beans
- Sliced jalapeños
- Diced tomatoes
- Sliced black olives
- Vegan sour cream
- Chopped fresh cilantro

**Instructions:**
1. Place tortilla chips on a platter that can go in the microwave.
2. Chips should be covered with vegan cheese slivers.
3. Thirty second intervals in the microwave until the cheese is melted.
4. Add cooked black beans, diced tomatoes, black olives, and jalapenos.
5. Serve with a garnish of chopped cilantro and vegan sour cream.

**Nutrition (per serving - 1 plate of nachos):**
- Calories: 350
- Fat: 15g
- Carbohydrates: 45g
- Fibre: 8g
- Protein: 10g

## VEGAN MEXICAN-INSPIRED SPEEDY TOFU SCRAMBLE:

*Ingredients:*
- Cooked and seasoned tofu scramble (see Tofu Scramble Breakfast Tacos recipe)
- Sliced avocado
- Salsa
- Whole wheat or gluten-free tortillas

*Instructions:*
1. Warm the cooked and seasoned tofu scramble.
2. Fill tortillas with tofu scramble, sliced avocado, and salsa.
3. Serve as breakfast tacos.

*Nutrition (per serving - 2 tacos):*
- Calories: 300
- Fat: 15g
- Carbohydrates: 30g
- Fibre: 8g
- Protein: 15g

## VEGAN MEXICAN-INSPIRED EXPRESS QUINOA BURRITO BOWL:

*Ingredients:*
- Cooked quinoa

- Cooked and seasoned black beans
- Sautéed bell peppers and onions
- Diced tomatoes
- Diced avocado
- Sliced black olives
- Vegan cheese shreds
- Vegan ranch dressing (see Creamy Chipotle Sauce recipe)
- Chopped fresh cilantro
- Lime wedges

**Instructions:**
1. Cooked quinoa, spiced black beans, sautéed bell peppers and onions, tomatoes, and avocado are combined in a bowl.
2. Black olive slices, vegan cheese crumbles, and vegan ranch dressing are sprinkled over the top.
3. Lime wedges and cilantro cut for garnish.

**Nutrition (per serving - 1 bowl):**
- Calories: 350
- Fat: 15g
- Carbohydrates: 45g
- Fibre: 10g
- Protein: 15g

## VEGAN MEXICAN-INSPIRED SPAGHETTI WITH SALSA MARINARA:

*Ingredients:*
- Cooked whole wheat or gluten-free spaghetti
- Salsa marinara (see Roasted Tomato Salsa recipe)
- Sautéed bell peppers and onions
- Diced tomatoes
- Chopped fresh cilantro
- Lime wedges

*Instructions:*
1. Put cooked pasta, marinara sauce, sautéed bell peppers, and onions in a pan.
2. Heat until well heated over medium heat.
3. Serve with lime wedges, cilantro, and tomato diced.

*Nutrition (per serving - 1 cup):*
- Calories: 250
- Fat: 5g
- Carbohydrates: 40g
- Fibre: 8g
- Protein: 10g

## VEGAN MEXICAN-INSPIRED SWEET POTATO AND BLACK BEAN QUESADILLA:

*Ingredients:*
- Cooked and mashed sweet potato
- Cooked and seasoned black beans
- Sautéed bell peppers and onions
- Vegan cheese shreds
- Whole wheat or gluten-free tortillas

*Instructions:*
1. Sweet potato should be mashed and spread over one-half of a tortilla.
2. On top, sprinkle vegan cheese crumbles, sautéed bell peppers, onions, and black beans.
3. The tortilla must be fried on a pan until crisp and browned after being folded in half.

*Nutrition (per serving - 1 quesadilla):*
- Calories: 300
- Fat: 10g
- Carbohydrates: 40g
- Fiber: 10g
- Protein: 10g

## VEGAN MEXICAN-INSPIRED JACKFRUIT SLOPPY JOES:

*Ingredients:*
- Cooked and seasoned jackfruit (see Jackfruit Carnitas Burritos recipe)
- Whole wheat or gluten-free hamburger buns
- Sliced red onion
- Sliced pickles

*Instructions:*
1. Warm the cooked and seasoned jackfruit.
2. Serve the jackfruit on hamburger buns and top with sliced red onion and pickles.

*Nutrition (per serving - 1 sandwich):*
- Calories: 300
- Fat: 5g
- Carbohydrates: 50g
- Fibre: 8g
- Protein: 10g

## VEGAN MEXICAN-INSPIRED BBQ CHICKPEA TACOS:

*Ingredients:*
- Cooked and seasoned chickpeas
- Whole wheat or gluten-free tortillas

- Sliced red onion
- Chopped fresh cilantro
- Lime wedges
- Vegan BBQ sauce

*Instructions:*
1. The seasoned, cooked chickpeas should be warmed.
2. Add chickpeas, red onion slices, and cilantro to the tortillas.
3. Serve with lime wedges and drizzle with vegan BBQ sauce.

*Nutrition (per serving - 2 tacos):*
- Calories: 300
- Fat: 5g
- Carbohydrates: 45g
- Fibre: 10g
- Protein: 10g

## VEGAN MEXICAN-INSPIRED TOFU NUGGETS WITH DIP:

*Ingredients:*
- Cooked and seasoned tofu nuggets (see Tofu and Vegetable Fajita Stir-Fry recipe)
- Vegan ranch dressing (see Creamy Chipotle Sauce recipe)

- Sliced carrots and cucumber

*Instructions:*
1. Serve the cooked and seasoned tofu nuggets with sliced carrots and cucumber.
2. Dip in vegan ranch dressing.

*Nutrition (per serving - 6 tofu nuggets with dip):*
- Calories: 250
- Fat: 10g
- Carbohydrates: 30g
- Fibre: 8g
- Protein: 15g

## VEGAN MEXICAN-INSPIRED CHEESY ZUCCHINI CASSEROLE:

*Ingredients:*
- Sliced zucchini
- Vegan cheese sauce (see Vegan Queso Fundido recipe)
- Mexican-inspired seasoning (chilli powder, cumin, paprika, garlic powder, onion powder, salt)

*Instructions:*
1. Sliced zucchini is arranged in a baking dish.
2. Over the zucchini, drizzle vegan cheese sauce.

3. Season with a bit of spice with a Mexican flair.
4. Bake for 20 to 25 minutes until bubbling and golden, at 375°F (190°C).

*Nutrition (per serving - 1 cup):*
- Calories: 200
- Fat: 10g
- Carbohydrates: 20g
- Fibre: 6g
- Protein: 10g

## VEGAN MEXICAN-INSPIRED STUFFED MUSHROOM CAPS:

*Ingredients:*
- Large mushroom caps
- Cooked and seasoned quinoa
- Sautéed bell peppers and onions
- Vegan cheese shreds
- Chopped fresh cilantro

*Instructions:*
1. An oven-safe baking dish should be lightly greased and heated to 375°F (190°C).
2. Fill mushroom caps with quinoa that has been cooked and seasoned, bell peppers, onions, and vegan cheese crumbles.

3. Bake the mushrooms for 15 to 20 minutes or until they are soft.
4. Before serving, garnish with chopped cilantro.

*Nutrition (per serving - 2 stuffed mushroom caps):*
- Calories: 250
- Fat: 10g
- Carbohydrates: 30g
- Fibre: 8g
- Protein: 10g

## VEGAN MEXICAN-INSPIRED POTATO AND POBLANO TACOS:

*Ingredients:*
- Cooked and seasoned potato cubes
- Roasted poblano pepper strips
- Whole wheat or gluten-free tortillas
- Vegan sour cream
- Chopped fresh cilantro

*Instructions:*
1. The roasted poblano pepper strips and cooked, seasoning-filled potato cubes are warmed.
2. Potato cubes and poblano pepper strips should be placed within tortillas.
3. Add chopped cilantro and vegan sour cream on top.

*Nutrition (per serving - 2 tacos):*
- Calories: 300
- Fat: 5g
- Carbohydrates: 45g
- Fibre: 8g
- Protein: 10g

## VEGAN MEXICAN-INSPIRED KID-FRIENDLY BURRITO BOWL:

*Ingredients:*
- Cooked and seasoned rice
- Cooked and seasoned black beans
- Vegan cheese shreds
- Sliced avocado
- Sliced black olives
- Vegan ranch dressing (see Creamy Chipotle Sauce recipe)
- Tortilla chips, crushed

*Instructions:*
1. Combine cooked rice, seasoned black beans, vegan cheese shreds, and sliced avocado in a bowl.
2. Top with sliced black olives, vegan ranch dressing, and crushed tortilla chips.

*Nutrition (per serving - 1 bowl):*
- Calories: 300

- Fat: 10g
- Carbohydrates: 40g
- Fibre: 10g
- Protein: 10g

## VEGAN MEXICAN-INSPIRED MINI TACO SALAD CUPS:

*Ingredients:*
- Mini tortilla cups
- Shredded lettuce
- Cooked and seasoned lentils or black beans
- Diced tomatoes
- Sliced black olives
- Vegan cheese shreds
- Vegan ranch dressing (see Creamy Chipotle Sauce recipe)
- Chopped fresh cilantro

*Instructions:*
1. Fill mini tortilla cups with shredded lettuce, cooked lentils or black beans, diced tomatoes, sliced black olives, and vegan cheese shreds.
2. Drizzle with vegan ranch dressing and garnish with chopped cilantro.

*Nutrition (per serving - 2 taco salad cups):*

- Calories: 200
- Fat: 5g
- Carbohydrates: 30g
- Fibre: 8g
- Protein: 10g

**Vegan Mexican-Inspired Stuffed Acorn Squash:**

**Ingredients:**
- Acorn squash, halved and seeds removed
- Cooked and seasoned black beans
- Sautéed bell peppers and onions
- Cooked quinoa
- Vegan cheese shreds
- Chopped fresh cilantro
- Lime wedges

**Instructions:**
1. Set the oven's temperature to 375°F (190°C).
2. Acorn squash halves should be placed cut side up on a baking pan.
3. Add cooked quinoa, black beans, sautéed bell peppers, and onions to each half of the pita.
4. Add vegan cheese slivers on top.
5. Bake the squash for 25 to 30 minutes or until it is soft.
6. Serve with lime wedges and cilantro that have been chopped.

*Nutrition (per serving - 1 stuffed acorn squash half):*
- Calories: 300
- Fat: 5g
- Carbohydrates: 50g
- Fiber: 12g
- Protein: 10g

## VEGAN MEXICAN-INSPIRED PORTOBELLO TACOS WITH CILANTRO PESTO:

**Ingredients:**
- Grilled portobello mushroom caps
- Whole wheat or gluten-free tortillas
- Shredded lettuce
- Diced tomatoes
- Vegan cilantro pesto (see Roasted Red Pepper and Walnut Dip recipe)
- Lime wedges

**Instructions:**
1. The portobello mushroom caps should be warmed up.
2. Shredded lettuce, diced tomatoes, and grilled portobello mushroom caps should be placed within tortillas.
3. Serve with lime wedges and vegan cilantro pesto drizzled over top.

**Nutrition (per serving - 2 tacos):**
- Calories: 250
- Fat: 10g
- Carbohydrates: 30g
- Fibre: 8g
- Protein: 10g

## VEGAN MEXICAN-INSPIRED EGGPLANT MOLE TOWER:

**Ingredients:**
- Grilled eggplant slices
- Vegan mole sauce (see Vegan Mole Poblano recipe)
- Sautéed bell peppers and onions
- Vegan cheese shreds
- Chopped fresh cilantro

**Instructions:**
1. Slices of grilled eggplant are layered with bell pepper, onion, and vegan cheese.
2. Add vegan mole sauce and drizzle.
3. Add chopped cilantro as a garnish.

**Nutrition (per serving - 1 tower):**
- Calories: 300
- Fat: 10g
- Carbohydrates: 40g
- Fibre: 10g

- Protein: 10g

## VEGAN MEXICAN-INSPIRED QUINOA-STUFFED BELL PEPPERS:

***Ingredients:***
- Bell peppers, tops removed and seeds removed
- Cooked quinoa
- Cooked and seasoned black beans
- Sautéed bell peppers and onions
- Diced tomatoes
- Vegan cheese shreds
- Chopped fresh cilantro

***Instructions:***
1. Set the oven's temperature to 375°F (190°C).
2. Fill bell peppers with black beans, chopped tomatoes, bell peppers, onions, and cooked quinoa.
3. Add vegan cheese slivers on top.
4. Bake the bell peppers for 20 to 25 minutes or until soft.
5. Before serving, garnish with chopped cilantro.

***Nutrition (per serving - 1 stuffed bell pepper):***
- Calories: 250
- Fat: 5g

- Carbohydrates: 40g
- Fibre: 10g
- Protein: 10g

## VEGAN MEXICAN-INSPIRED LENTIL SHEPHERD'S PIE WITH MASHED CAULIFLOWER:

*Ingredients:*
- Cooked and seasoned lentils
- Sautéed bell peppers and onions
- Vegan cheese shreds
- Mashed cauliflower (see Vegan Cauliflower Mashed Potatoes recipe)
- Chopped fresh cilantro

*Instructions:*
1. Set the oven's temperature to 375°F (190°C).
2. Layer cooked lentils, sautéed bell peppers, onions, and vegan cheese crumbs in a baking dish.
3. Add mashed cauliflower on top.
4. Bake until bubbling and brown, about 20 to 25 minutes.
5. Before serving, garnish with chopped cilantro.

*Nutrition (per serving - 1 cup):*
- Calories: 250

- Fat: 5g
- Carbohydrates: 40g
- Fibre: 10g
- Protein: 10g

## VEGAN MEXICAN-INSPIRED TEMPEH FAJITAS WITH SMOKY PAPRIKA SAUCE:

**Ingredients:**
- Cooked and seasoned tempeh strips
- Sautéed bell peppers and onions
- Whole wheat or gluten-free tortillas
- Smoky paprika sauce (see Chipotle Black Bean Soup recipe)
- Chopped fresh cilantro
- Lime wedges

**Instructions:**
1. The prepared and seasoned tempeh strips, bell peppers, and onions have been sautéed.
2. Bell peppers, onions, and tempeh strips should be placed within tortillas.
3. Serve with lime wedges and cilantro that have been chopped. Drizzle with smoky paprika sauce.

**Nutrition (per serving - 2 fajitas):**

- Calories: 300
- Fat: 10g
- Carbohydrates: 30g
- Fiber: 8g
- Protein: 15g

## VEGAN MEXICAN-INSPIRED CHICKPEA AND SPINACH ENCHILADAS:

*Ingredients:*
- Cooked and seasoned chickpeas
- Sautéed bell peppers and onions
- Baby spinach
- Whole wheat or gluten-free tortillas
- Enchilada sauce (see Spicy Salsa Verde recipe)
- Vegan cheese shreds
- Chopped fresh cilantro

*Instructions:*
1. Set the oven's temperature to 375°F (190°C).
2. Layer cooked chickpeas, bell peppers, onions, and baby spinach in each tortilla.
3. The tortillas should be rolled up and put in a baking tray.

4. Then, sprinkle vegan cheese shards on top of the tortillas after adding enchilada sauce.
5. Bake the dish for 20 to 25 minutes or until the cheese bubbles and melts.
6. Before serving, garnish with chopped cilantro.

**Nutrition (per serving - 2 enchiladas):**
- Calories: 300
- Fat: 10g
- Carbohydrates: 40g
- Fiber: 10g
- Protein: 15g

## VEGAN MEXICAN-INSPIRED RATATOUILLE TACOS:

**Ingredients:**
- Ratatouille (see Vegan Ratatouille recipe)
- Whole wheat or gluten-free tortillas
- Vegan cheese shreds
- Chopped fresh cilantro

**Instructions:**
1. Warm the ratatouille.
2. Fill tortillas with ratatouille and vegan cheese shreds.
3. Garnish with chopped cilantro before serving.

*Nutrition (per serving - 2 tacos):*
- Calories: 250
- Fat: 5g
- Carbohydrates: 40g
- Fibre: 10g
- Protein: 8g

## VEGAN MEXICAN-INSPIRED STUFFED ARTICHOKES WITH ROASTED RED PEPPER SAUCE:

*Ingredients:*
- Cooked and seasoned quinoa
- Sautéed bell peppers and onions
- Cooked and seasoned black beans
- Stuffed artichoke hearts (see Vegan Stuffed Artichokes recipe)
- Roasted red pepper sauce (see Roasted Red Pepper and Walnut Dip recipe)
- Chopped fresh cilantro

*Instructions:*
1. Stuffed artichoke hearts should be added to prepared quinoa, sautéed bell peppers, onions, and seasoned black beans.
2. Add roasted red pepper sauce as a drizzle.
3. Before serving, garnish with chopped cilantro.

*Nutrition (per serving - 2 stuffed artichokes):*

- Calories: 300
- Fat: 5g
- Carbohydrates: 40g
- Fibre: 10g
- Protein: 10g

## VEGAN MEXICAN-INSPIRED PORTOBELLO MUSHROOM STEAKS WITH CHIMICHURRI:

*Ingredients:*
- Grilled portobello mushroom caps
- Chimichurri sauce (see Cilantro Lime Crema recipe)
- Sliced red onion
- Chopped fresh cilantro

*Instructions:*
1. The portobello mushroom caps should be warmed up.
2. Add some chimichurri sauce.
3. Add chopped cilantro and red onion slices on top.

*Nutrition (per serving - 1 mushroom steak):*
- Calories: 150
- Fat: 5g
- Carbohydrates: 10g

- Fibre: 4g
- Protein: 8g

## Conclusion:

Conclusion 1: Honoring Custom and Kindness We hope that by the time we have finished our tour of Mexican cuisine, you will have enjoyed the satisfaction of tasting the union of compassion and tradition. You've demonstrated that it's possible to respect culinary tradition while simultaneously making moral decisions that lead to a more sustainable future by picking products derived from plants. Your culinary creations are now a part of this rich fabric, just as Mexican cuisine is a tapestry woven with history, culture, and colourful ingredients. Remember that every bite you consume is a small step towards a kinder, more peaceful world as you explore the recipes in this cookbook and try out your kitchen experiments. Second conclusion: Kitchen to the World I'm happy you've finished the book "Vibrant Flavors: A Vegan Journey Through Mexican Cuisine." But this is only the start! These recipes can spread beyond your kitchen and reach out to friends, family, and other people. Share the inspirations behind each recipe, the skills you've honed, and your newly discovered love for the ingredients on your table. You're not simply cooking when you share these recipes and your experiences; you're also a spokesperson for combining Mexican culinary tradition with contemporary plant-based living. Let's ignite a worldwide movement that celebrates diversity of taste, culture, and compassion in every mouthwatering morsel. Conclusion 3: A Snack for the Future, a Taste of Mexico We wish you well as you finish this cookbook and move on to new culinary explorations while bringing the vivid spirit of Mexico with you. More than just a cookbook, "Vibrant Flavors" has been a voyage through time-honoured customs and celebrating the elegance of a plant-based lifestyle. Your taste senses will never forget the flavour of Mexico, which will serve as a constant reminder to put more sustainability, compassion, and flavour into everything you cook. May the dishes in this cookbook provide joy, connection, and a sense of purpose to your kitchen for years to come, from celebratory celebrations to warm family dinners? 4. Conclusion Good Practice: Savor Each BiteRemember that Mexican food's charm and plant-based ingredients' potency are always available as you relish the final tastes of your gastronomic journey. Your journey is not simply a one-time event; it is a way of life that honours the love of food, the joy of cooking, and the reverence for all living things. May you discover fulfilment, creativity, and a profound connection to the world around you with each dish you cook from "Vibrant Flavors: A Vegan Journey Through Mexican Cuisine." So take a deep breath, lift your fork, and relish each excellent, kind bite. Happy Prosperity!

# The End

Printed in Great Britain
by Amazon